SALES AND SELLING YOURSELF

IF YOU CAN MAKE SOMEONE LAUGH, THEY CAN BE YOURS

RICK BREITWEISER

CONTENTS

BUSINESS SALES AND SALESMANSHIP

HUMOR

HAPPINESS

ACKNOWLEDGEMENTS

Chris & Lisa, Mary B, Tommy & Sue, Ralph M., Nick & Joyce,
Charlie & Patty, the Breitweisers, and the Kellys, & Gary Y.

PREFACE

Success is a relative concept. It's not the same for any two people. What works for you might not work for someone else. But what really matters is how you push yourself to become the best version of yourself every day. Perhaps we have been gifted with a certain charisma or a healthy confidence level. Or just charming enough to influence the flow of thinking or chemistry we have with others? However, if even after honing your skillset, you fall short of pitching and selling yourself, it is all for naught. You need to retain your authenticity and leave a mark on others. We know it's not as easy as it seems, but don't worry; we will peel back the layers one at a time as we move ahead with the book. When you get down to the essence of it, everyone has an artistic composition, or let's call it an art form. It is inside each of us, waiting to be freed It can be in any form: a story, a poem, a song, a painting, or anything expressive. We all carry the bits and pieces of our journey and experience with us, every breathing moment. For some, this art might stem from their curiosity about the world or their acceptance of it. Some might want to muse over the most memorable of times in their life. For others, their artform could be an aftermath of an event, a period of time, or a significant chapter in their life. Whether brilliant or mundane, this composition can be found in almost every human being, as we can argue that everyone has their own story to narrate to the world. Yet, it is not everyone's story the world gets to witness and stare at in wonder.

Some people are willing to share what is inside them and want to voice their most profound thoughts in some way or another. Others think differently. They believe it is too personal for the world to know, or maybe they are just afraid of how it will sound to others. It is okay if you fall into the category of people who wish for their art and story to remain only theirs. It can stay all yours if you wish it that way. Your thoughts and your emotions are safe without action. But if you want to break out of your inner doors and no longer want to be afraid to express yourself, this book is for you.

Feelings are free but may be costly if they're wasted, which is why this book aims to guide you in presenting yourself in the right direction. You will start a journey, a mission, but one you must complete. If you accept this mission, remember words don't write themselves; you will have to put in your share of efforts. This book aims to therapeutically exercise your mind and will finally let only your creative way s have a say in narrating its story. Throughout the pages of this book, I make it a point to speak directly to you, to "show you the way" to truly sell yourself to the world.

Now, before we even begin learning the true steps to achieve the end result, you need to know what this book is trying to tell. Now I know many eyebrows might shoot up at "selling yourself" in a positive connotation, so even before we begin, let me clarify the concept: 'Selling yourself' is all about doing anything the way you do it, completely unique only and only to you. It is a depiction of your worthiness to others. Selling yourself is about putting forth the best "you" for the entire world to see and being confident that they will accept you.

But we cannot ignore that doing so is a scary idea. If you were to put yourself out there, you also have to open yourself to a lot of questions and feedback. You begin by pondering, "Who am I to you? Who am I to the rest of the world? What do others see in me? Why are there people in this world who are so accepted and appreciated by others? How do I become one of them while keeping my style and integrity intact?"

All of these questions are valid and precisely the ones I have addressed in the book. These concerns are looming in our minds and forming a war though there is a lot of work to be done to find the ultimate answer—all of those things are covered in the chapters ahead the beginning of your journey will always be from the truth—your truth. To find the answer and ultimately "sell yourself" to the world, you must begin by representing the ever-cherished quality of truth. Together, we will achieve all that.

We intend to get into the psyche of your character. As of today, when I say you are the main character, the protagonist, who runs the world and makes the most of your status, it is time you start understanding it as much as possible. As you process through the chapters further, you will come face to face with yourself via different fields and subsets—areas of psychology, character, human nature, sense of humor, spirituality, as well as business and salesmanship. The goal of the book is for you to learn something new about yourself via each of these stages.

However, before we begin, let me warn you about this one-of-a-kind adventurous trip you are about to pledge yourself towards. Though designed to enlighten your core, this book does not come easy. Every lesson will come with a challenge of its own, and there is a pattern of redundancies with repeated phrases. But don't be alarmed, they come to you as reminders when you least expect them, acting as a way of constant reinforcement of the most important topics you are to cover. Some chapters are long, driving the point into your mind with a drill, and some will be short, giving you instruction and trusting you enough that you will follow. There will be a lot of twists and turns because when has the journey to self-discovery and when has the acceptance been easy? But with every turn, a new view will be revealed, a new way you will look in the mirror. So, get your business suit on, briefcase dusted and stuffed because the journey from discovering yourself to finally selling yourself is starting!

DISCOVERY AND INVENTING YOURSELF

CHAPTER 1

MARKETING YOURSELF

"For you, you are the easiest thing to market,
put yourself out there where they can see you."

It was in 1983 that I was taking a class by Professor Tchir on marketing. For the world, Mr. Tchir was a marketing executive for NCR, but for me, he was an incredible teacher. Why? Simple—because I never forgot anything that was ever taught in his class. However, I also clearly remember getting a B- in all the assignments I ever handed in to him. I asked Tony, who usually sat next to me, whether I could look at his papers to see what I might do better. I saw a glaring, obvious pattern in every single one of them. His assignments had an A at the end of the last page. Yes, the last page! His was always a stapled report, unlike mine, which was summed up in a single sheet, adorning not a single stapler pin. I went through his answers to find that none of his works had an upper edge over mine, scholastically or intellectually. My approach to all of the answers had been to make a point and conclude, but not Tony, who believed in fattening up his reports with a little bit of everything here and there, thus adding more pages. It pains me to add "fluff", unless it's on a peanut butter sandwich! But I digress, my answers had more brevity, depth, and accuracy as they talked about what was actually asked. Yet to Mr. Tchir, more pages signaled more effort, and Tony's share of "more" ultimately overpowered mine. Having cracked the case, the decision was now up to me: should I stick to the way of the student whose grade was in someone else's hands, or should I turn to the way of the professor to whom I was marketing my paper, and buy a stapler? For the rest of the semester, I made some "half-time" adjustments, and, in the end, got a B+ as my final grade.

Though the incident might not have gotten me a better grade than Tony, it taught me a valuable lesson that I never forgot. Just like I never forgot Professor Tchir's definition of marketing—"Getting the right product, to the right market, at the right time, with the right price, and the right profit is marketing." Odd, huh? His definition was brief and accurate, so I would have given him an A if I were the teacher, but would he give himself one if we were to go by his more-words-mean-more-effort approach? Nonetheless, he did teach me a valuable lesson, as I said. That marketing is in every single part of your existence. How you behave in the world and how people perceive is nothing less than the result of you "marketing" yourself to them, whether you do it consciously or not.

Tony had marketed himself as a hardworking student who researched more and wrote more (cue to his stapled assignments), yet I had marketed myself as not-so-hardworking with my one-paged assignment that did not showcase the same vigor. Selling yourself is the same as marketing yourself, and it is marketing 101 to know that if you want positive results, approach the audience in the way that will reach them most favourably. If I had continued writing one-paged assignments, perhaps my grade would have been B- or C my entire semester, but if I had caught on to the way that spoke the most to Mr. Tchir from the very beginning, I might have gotten a higher grade than Tony. This is usually not my way. I tend to be outspoken and unreceptive; appeasement is not even in my dictionary. Yet my wise mind steps in here and reminds me that I am a winner at all ethical costs.

Marketing yourself or selling yourself is all about controlling people's initial perceptions of you. You are a brand in yourself, and if you want to successfully market your brand, you have to know your audience. If you don't, someone else, the Tonys of your life, will catch on quicker than you do, earning a more favourable outcome than you do.

CHAPTER 2

IT JUST COMES NATURALLY

*"Quick wittedness requires quick thinking...
something practice can't improve."*

Human beings have many qualities that make them stand out from the crowd, allowing others to notice them. You might be smart, good-looking, intelligent, etc., but one personality trait that appeals the most to almost everyone is being naturally funny and quick-witted. Though the sad reality is that these innate qualities are distinctive, found only in a few. Of course, other attributes, too, shine on their own, but it is the sense of humor that is rarely forgotten or left out.

Being quick-witted and funny are natural qualities, hardly to be mimicked. And I have always thought of myself as a funny guy, for which I credit my creative gene. When you are a deep thinker, dreamer, inventor, or even a teacher or instructor, you can see what's coming in a conversation and easily lead it in the direction you want. The more knowledgeable you are, the more you possess to draw from. Knowledge is power, and you already know that, but it is also social. With knowledge comes intuition. I have somewhat of an ability to read people. I will put myself in the shoes of those before me and play both roles, meaning that

I can sense what I think the other person wants or expects to hear. If you, too, have this ability, you can make someone feel at ease or nervous. You can make the situation awkward or pleasant, and the best is making someone laugh, a sure shot way of gaining their amiability.

But be aware! Being funny is no funny business, as it is purely to be led by its naturalness. It has to aid in a free-flowing conversation, not to be inserted forcefully to make someone awkward. There is a fine line between being funny and annoying; you must know when to pull back. Unfortunately, it takes years to master this skill. So, if you know you are not funny, or your joke will be met with a look of befuddlement well, my friend, it's time to change your strategies and explore more of your humorous side before presenting it to others. Sadly, do not try this at home!

Did you ever notice when you are in the company of someone funny enough to make you laugh can uplift you from a bad day?

A WAKE-UP AWAKENING

*"The hardest things to see are
the ones your brain doesn't."*

Every Friday night in the 80s, I was a regular in the New Jersey or NYC nightclub scene, along with my best bud Tommy. We were part of a non-distinct, slightly larger group, but he and I were always in attendance. I used to say …"there are 52 Fridays a year, and I ain't missing one of them"!

On one of these nights, I remember, I had my eyes set on a pretty girl whose effortless charm drew me in instantly. Knowing what a sucker I was for redheads, I made my way straight to her, slipping past the crowd with my Tanqueray and tonic in hand. I was determined to hit it off with her. I had set my hopes high, as I usually did, and was already getting into "confident Rick" to seem more appealing. I always looked confident on the outside, outside being the keyword here. But every time I would turn on the false confidence to talk to some girl, Tommy would check in with a "Who's your new friend?", and all the attention would be on him. I could see it coming, like lava from a volcano. I would only be so surprised if I could only manage to stave off his charming ways with my new find. That turned out to be wishful thinking. In only a matter of minutes, both laughed, and maybe me too, but only to myself. That was enough to know there had to be someone else to come into my life that night. Well, the night is still young, and so am I, and I can find someone else. It wasn't like I was looking to get married on a Friday night.

Tommy would add another-worldly aura to the conversation. He made people laugh, especially girls. No matter what the situation—a nightclub, the beach, a bar, a restaurant, indoors or outdoors, it didn't matter because my friend would always be the one who could charm the girls. Everyone around me always told me that women loved funny guys. And that very same bunch also said I was one of them. I already told you about the significance of the charm of being funny in the previous chapter. I have always considered quick-wittedness and a good sense of humor to be my best friends. So, where's my Heidi Klum?

A good part of our learning comes from experience and observing others. Tommy's ways eventually woke up something in me. Like a revelation or an awakening, I realized that he, or possibly anyone else, could display unwavering courage and less afraid of failure. But with the many attributes I'm already aware of, nothing should stand in the way of feeling more proud of myself and what I have to offer. My lack of confidence is truly unfounded and doesn't need suppression. I lacked self-confidence and never really knew how to accept, embrace, and love myself. But that was not the case with Tommy. He, on the other hand, eluded an air of confidence and self-worth. Combined with funny, that sounds like a better deal to any girl.

I had always had low self-esteem and thought of myself as of lesser value in any conversation. I feared acceptance, which stemmed from having a father who was always difficult to please. My low self-esteem and issues regarding self-confidence hindered many of my conversations, something not even a good sense of humor could save. If you "force it," it shows, and that can never work in your favor. Such situations often lead to total embarrassment.

Once I learned this truth, I knew it was time to change my ways. If I wanted to leave an impression on a girl or anyone else in the world, I needed my self-doubts to stop overpowering my mind. I needed to learn not to give into my self-limited beliefs, which only held me down in the end.

You might find yourself in situations where you too will underestimate your worth. And some of these situations can really cost you a lot. By putting yourself down and not owning up to the confidence you should carry yourself with, you are limiting how much can truly be achieved by you. Tommy taught me, via bitter defeats, that I should not sell myself short. If I carried myself confidently, everyone around me would be lured in automatically. So, you, too, stop setting limits on yourself and your confidence. Do not cage yourself; ultimately, be afraid of putting the true you out there. If you believe you deserve something, go for it, and the entire world will believe in you.

CHAPTER 4

JUDGING WAYS AND PERSPECTIVE

*"When something about you bothers me,
I judge you. It may be natural, but it's not OK."*

As a human, it is in your nature to be overly judgmental. And, of course, this judgment is based on your first impression of someone, whether it is via their appearance or action. At the initial encounter, you can't see the true depths of someone's character., As a result, you are more likely to end up with an unfair evaluation of their entire being. Yet, you cannot help it.

"Don't judge a book by its cover!"—you might have heard and read this a million times in your life. The fundamental essence is that you should not conclude without having all the facts or contempt to a prior investigation. Someone could very well be kind and generous, but maybe you catch them on a bad day and are convinced that they are terrible. Then, before all is known, you end up with unfortunate miscalculations, leading to incorrect conclusions. So, yes, the saying, however cliché it might sound, is true. But even when you know all of this and have been taught so many times, your mind wants to jump to conclusions… it's a habit!

And usually, when the mind rushes to these conclusions, there are two ways it can go in its approach: either you will do so by comparing YOURSELF to others, "yourself" here being the positive standard to be met, or conversely, you will end up comparing SOMEONE ELSE (others)to you, viewing yourself in a negative light. As in, I am jealous or envious of you in some way. In either case, although a natural tendency, this book brings awareness to patterns of loving yourself for who you are, thus minimizing the compulsion to judge others so much, which is critical and wrong.

Mark Twain famously said, "What other people think of me is none of my business." Although it is very profound, I believe the statement has two sides. On the one hand, it preaches that you cannot control what someone else thinks of you, so why even bother worrying about it? But on the other hand, it presents a different meaning altogether. If you know what others think of you, you can take it positively and use it to assess yourself. If you know, you can use it to your advantage, making it easier for you to improve yourself and fix any flaws you might have. It will act as a mirror to yourself, allowing you to see yourself as you truly are.

But even such a comparison is a double-edged sword. You might consider what is being said to you and even start comparing yourself to the person who said it and to everyone around you. But what you might forget is that the surrounding that has shaped you is not the same as that person's. In most cases, you fail to take the circumstances into consideration. Some people might not have parents, or some might not even have a home. The situations they grew up in and lived in might be way different than the ones you faced, whether for the better or worse, which means that the person those circumstances shaped will also be different. Some might have faced many hardships in life, making them more equipped to deal with challenging situations. And there might be people who have been pampered since birth, turning them into dependent beings. Life can teach you a lot—from making you want to learn from your mistakes to giving you the ability to differentiate right from wrong. And with these life lessons, you create your character, which is why every character molded is different.

Someone who is ill-mannered probably knows no manners. In contrast, one who has been instilled with them has been outfitted with them. Instilled and outfitted doesn't mean everyone remembers them or rank highly with them either.

So, before you stand in front of someone and judge them, or even when you judge yourself in comparison, remember all of this. Remember that everyone's path is different, so everyone's journey would also be different. If you want to judge someone, remember to only do that once you have all the facts; it is only fair. And since, I am guessing, you aren't a mind reader, the probability of you being easily wrong is very high, especially when you wrongly jump to conclusions. Remember all of this the next time your mind jumps ahead of you.

NOT A LEVEL-PLAYING FIELD

*Not being better than someone, but being
better at something than someone doesn't
make you a better human being.*

A lot of people out there love to complain that life is unfair, and maybe some people actually saying so are right. Yet, His creation is miraculously assembled to function as it does until it doesn't. Someday you and everyone around you will all be gone, and the planet would still be hanging around in space as it was before everyone arrived. Well, unless God calls for another big meteor!

Take the example of any race, whether it is of horses, humans, or even cars driven by NASCAR drivers. They all go around an oval track. Before the race begins, all of them are to be assembled at the starting point. The horses must be at the gates, side-by-side, from right to left, beginning closest to the inside rail. For the human runners, they are to be at the starting blocks in their assigned lanes, with the outer most lanes fanned further down the track. And in the case of a car race, the road is only wide enough to accommodate the width of 2 cars at a time, side-by-side in a parade of slow-moving pairs when they start. In any of these races, the case usually is that compensation is devised because the distance for the most inside lanes are shorter distance than the wider turns made by the outer lanes. So, if you are positioned in the middle, it means that your distance is further down the track than the lanes to your left, closer to the infield (all races run counterclockwise). Since some players might end up earning this advantage, a lot of sporting events use track record, where they call this advantage 'seeding.' A better seed or an advantage is awarded to the best record-holders. So far, nothing works better and is widely used in all sports. But if even games offer these advantages, what about life?

So life can be unfair, but this unfairness is not irreversible. Someone else might have a slight advantage over you at the beginning of the race, but they won't win if you're faster than them. In the end, what matters, in the long run, isn't the easy route but what one achieves with whatever road is available. Life is 10% what is given to you and 90% about what you achieve with it. Your attitude shapes the course of your journey; it decides if you want to run or if you want to not enter the race at all.

Have you or someone you know ever received special treatment because of their looks or brains? Have you ever been preferred for something because of the one picking liked you the most? Or maybe you were rejected because they didn't like you at all? Of course, that's the way things go. Our life is full of such instances. We see the world falling at the feet of a celebrity just because they are famous. Even the sons and daughters of famous parents get first looks and preferential treatment because their parents or relatives have already made it big. The same cannot be said about an aspiring actor from a small town in the Midwest who said, "I'm going to Hollywood to make it big."

"It Never Rains in Southern California"—Albert Hammond

CHAPTER 6

YOU'RE EXACTLY YOU

"I am a rebel, but a good rebel.
The best part about being me is I get to be exactly me."

I'm allowed to believe in whatever I choose. Some of us are deep thinkers, and since such is the case with me, I must uncover and get to the bottom of everything to walk away satisfied. If I don't understand how a cam shaft works, then I'll never know what the lifters do either solid or hydraulic. It's who I am.

Free will is a pass to be me. To follow my God-given instincts every wakening minute.

Some might reach this conclusion by researching humanity for years, or some might say it is so because they do not have an opposing truth. Some people say everything is pre-planned and we have no free will at all. Their own mantra is usually used to deal with these diverse opinions. Everyone has their theories, including me.

One of my ideas about life and human existence was formed a while ago. I asked a good friend, who I consider very intelligent, about his views of how we are as humans when we come into this world. He believed everyone is born neutral with a clean slate and an unadulterated unimpressed mind. Though I respected his belief, I strongly disagreed with him.

I believe that each human is designed to think the way I do, whereas all of us are created on slightly different levels, with variations predisposed in our brains. Observations can be made…people are happy, or they are not. They can be sad, too. People can be funny because they are inherently funny, and some try their best, but everyone around them can see that it is an act. Some of them might even have resources like intelligence, personality, or finance to overcome them, and some might have no help at all.

I was once acquainted with someone I found intolerable as most of her social skills revolved around interjecting someone else in the middle of a conversation to be heard. Yes, I found it quite annoying, as much as the next person would, but I also realized that this was who she was, and there was little I could have done to change her. You cannot change people completely, not even yourself. You are who you are, and are limited to how much you can do to change that. The world might teach you lessons or tell you to go the way everyone else is going, but your inner disposition remains as it was, whether good or bad. You can only be you, whosoever that is.

"Please me by liking me, or please just don't like me."

Everyone's thought-process and even thoughts are different. Some are genuinely good people, and then there are evil ones. Every time something goes wrong, we wonder why these evil people exist and blame God for putting them among us. We can try to find a reason as to why they exist, but we can only theorize. But no matter what, my initial point remains that the world is filled with people you might not understand, but they exist nonetheless.

Some are gifted with unique minds, like Albert Einstein, Beethoven, Nikola Tesla, Marie Curie, and others. And then there is the rest of the population. Many people have intrusive thoughts. Some act upon them, and some choose to suppress them. Some, like Walt Disney, Thomas Edison, and Isaac Newton, were chastised by society in their early days but were some of the greatest minds that ever walked this planet.

CHAPTER 7

LEADING THE SPOTLIGHT

"All the World's a Stage"—William Shakespeare

These words by Shakespeare showcase that all of humanity, even you, the one reading it, and I, the one writing it, are actors. You are assigned your roles daily, whether a mother, father, teacher, dentist, stranger, etc. Of course, your role is not static; it keeps fluctuating with the passage of time, but the point remains that all are actors in the play of the world. And a lot about you can be determined by how well you play this role and how you present yourself to the world.

On my 18th birthday, a few friends took me to see the White Tiger band at the famous Soap Factory in Palisades Park, NJ. We had to wait in a long line to get in, the place was fully packed. It was my first experience being in a nightclub, and I was surprised to see that the beers were $1; any liquor store outside was selling a 6-pack for $2.10. Nonetheless, I pushed to the stage area and saw the most beautiful sight. Beautiful girls were bopping, bouncing, and swooning over the band. They couldn't possibly all be sisters! I looked at the rockstars on the stage and completely understood their admiration—they looked so cool. At that moment, I pledged, "I must become a rock star." The very next day,

I bought an electric guitar and began to let my hair grow. Unfortunately, I was already accepted to college as a pre-med student, but I still play the guitar daily to this day.

Thirty-five years later, White Tiger did a reunion tour in New Jersey, and I connected with them as a close friend's band opened their showcase. I had a conversation with the lead singer Neil Thomas. I said I remember the first song, the first time I saw your band when I was 18. "Ain't That A Shame" by Cheap Trick.

These guys played everything just like the record. I can see why all the girls there dug these long-haired rock stars. They were incredible showmen. It reminds me of Van Halen, who was just making a name for themselves at the time. Seeing them perform again, even after so much time had passed, was no different. I could still see the same brilliance in them, the same "coolness" my 18-year-old self had found in them. They were not only exceptional on the stage but just as likeable in real life, which is probably why people loved them as artists and celebrities, not just as mere musicians who were forgotten the minute they stepped down.

Over the years, my career took me on several different paths, some that were familiar to me and others where everything was new. At every stage, I met new people, faced new challenges, and had to present a different side of myself. Yet, at each stage, I remembered the band my 18-year-old saw and was determined to do everything with the same determination they performed on stage. No matter what walk of life, I wanted to give it my best, and that is exactly what you should also aim to do.

Create your brand, yourself, and your stage. Every waking moment of your life is a performance, and an award for it you must win. Be inclusive, have class, good manners, moral principles, and fairness; give everything your all because you never know when an 18-year-old is watching you and is being inspired by you.

CHAPTER 8

IMAGERY VS. HONESTY

"Your conscience is light when you're honest."

IF I WERE TO WRITE A screenplay where all personality traits would be personified, I would pick Honesty as my protagonist. This is because honesty plays a huge part in all our lives, as it should. It did the same for me because it was a part of everything I have done my entire life. Not lying to someone, not cheating, not stealing is honesty—so honesty has been a part of every scene of my life.

I am sure a lot of you use truth and honesty interchangeably. However, both concepts have distinguishable differences. Honesty is at the top of any sheet of paper, like Babe Ruth in Right Field! And because of leeway and not absolutism, misinterpretation of the truth is sometimes not acceptable or even possible, but such is not the case with honesty, is it? Someone once told me that "taking money from the cash register and admitting it when you get caught is the truth, and putting it back before getting caught and realizing what you did is honesty". While I appreciated their distinction, the discrimination between the two has always been a bit heavier. For me, honesty is not even taking money that is not yours in the first place.

When the question comes to selling anything and selling yourself, this phenomenon of truth and honesty is the trickiest to handle. In the marketing world, you will often find people who fabricate something without any evidence of truth, creating a facade or imagery that is not truthful and is dishonest. Then, they will create beautiful ads for a product, claiming it does so much. In the beginning, they might even woo people with their big claims and bigger illusions, gaining a lot of support and hype, but as soon as the product is bought and used, people will know the truth. They will be aware of all the funny business and never return to the product again.

Selling yourself works in a very similar way. If the entire world is your stage, it is your TV. You are giving a performance, and yes, you will convince everyone else that you are good at what you do, but sadly, this is not something you can enact, not for long anyway. This is why when the question comes to selling yourself and making a name for yourself. It is always best to take an honest tact.

Accepting a loss today for what it is will build integrity and an honest character that will pay off tomorrow. Many times in life, you will be reminded that integrity is the foundation of a good character, and it is true. So, it's logical to assume that integrity can't exist without an honest living, and vice versa. And despite having dishonest tendencies buried inside our core, it is paramount to our[A26] cause for success to replace our wicked ways of thought with righteous ones when they emerge. When we live an honest lifestyle, we strengthen our character. Our character on this world's stage becomes who it is meant to be, giving a peek into our reality to everyone around us.

Similarly, if we are authentic, we will attract authenticity. If we are not, everyone around us will see right through. Dishonesty might be ingrained in us because it is human nature after all, but it is up to us to not let it seep into the depths of our souls. It will cause cracks in our character and, ultimately, in the way everyone around perceives us. It will do nothing but erode and destroy our character, and if we lose it, we will lose a part of ourselves and our true potential.

PERSONAL TRAITS

CHAPTER 9

CHARACTER VS. PERSONALITY, INSIDE AND OUT

"If you are charming, go charm someone.
Snake charmers, or people charmers.
It's all about having their attention."

MARTIN LUTHER KING SAID, "I HAVE a dream that my four little children will one day live in a nation where they will not be judged by the color of their skin but by the content of their character." So, if one of the greatest minds ever lived tells us to focus on the character inside, why can't we? Though his struggles were greater than just the idea of character, he was right to point out that the only way humans should ever be judged is based on who they truly are, not what they look like or any other superficial factor.

But usually, when we talk of character and the kind of person we are on the inside, we intermix this concept with our "personality." Ask the person sitting next to you, and they will probably say that a character and a personality are the same, but I want you to let go of this belief immediately. Character and Personality are not the same concepts, though they might be a little similar in the sense that they are related to humans.

Your brain can usually be considered your body's hardware, whereas the mind can be counted as the software. Things relating to your mind exist and originate in the depths of the brain. So, things like emotions, feelings, and thoughts are all related to your mind, and as a result, to your character. Your character is essentially determined by every single feeling that your mind experiences and displays, whether good or unpleasant. Generous, truthful, goofy, selfish, greedy, dishonest, etc.—all of them are a part of your true character. These traits might not be visible to you from the beginning, but you start noticing them over time.

On the other hand, personality includes the traits that hover outside your brain, not deep inside. These traits might be a little too obvious from the get-go, like being funny, anxious, rude, confident, etc. They are easy to detect as personality traits, and they are also clearly visible by our actions.

Another way of telling them apart is by knowing that character traits are objective, not open for discussion, and come from within your mind. You are either generous or you are not. You are either honest or you are not, selfish or not. They jump from within your consciousness, even before your brain catches on and intuitively knows how to act. Personality traits, on the other side of the swing, are subjective. For example, I think Bob Newhart is a great comedian, but my friend does not think so, so that is "subjective" or debatable. In short, character revolves around integrity, fidelity, compassion, contribution, and responsibility, whereas personality revolves around image creation, public relations, communication, and management skills…the things that are outwardly obvious through one's actions.

I've always considered myself shy, but almost every person I have met says they think I am very confident. I think I am less confident than shy because I am shy on the inside, but my level of confidence is evident in my behavior on my exterior. This tells you how characters and personality traits differ from each other, but also, know that pitching one against the other does not mean that one is superior or the other is inferior. Your character matters as much as your personality when it comes to selling yourself and making yourself happy. You need both, but to utilise both, you need to know which is which. Now that you know, I hope you will use them fully.

Personality	Character
Personality is the way one carries oneself.	Character is what a person is like inside.
Different things such as sense of humor, friendliness, and passions determine your personality.	Major components of your character include honesty, respect, responsibility, courage, and loyalty (or the contrary of these).
Personality is connected with someone's appearance and characteristics that make them unique.	Character encompasses one's moral values.
Personality is subjective.	Character is objective.

CHAPTER 10

LAW OF UNATTRACTION

*"Don't let your ego control your looks.
It will always end up ugly."*

"That person is so ugly!"—whenever you hear this sentence, the first thing that comes to mind is that the person being talked about is physically unattractive. "Ugly," in our minds, refers to how someone looks, and that is how most of people in this world think. But it should not be like this. "Ugliness" stands to be a strong word and should rather talk of what kind of a person someone is, not just based on how someone looks. If I were to hear someone saying, "that person is so ugly!", I would relate it to the shallowness of their character. Even when I talk of someone being attractive, the qualities I see in them are them being likable and loveable, not just the beauty of their skin and appearance. Imagine a world where we could turn everyone inside out. In a world where we would judge someone based on who they are as a person, not on what they look like. If this were to happen, imagine how many beautiful people you might see around you, people you might have missed in the past because you were too focused on their outer appearance!

Don't let that bother you, and it's in our nature as humans to focus primarily on looks. I guess it's God's way of instilling judgment in all of us. And like we discussed a few chapters ago, being judgmental is simply comparing yourself to someone else or comparing someone else to yourself. So yes, it is not that much of an endearing quality, and frankly, it stands to be the definition of 'ugly.'

Think about it. How many times has someone attractive caught your eye? A lot of times, I am sure, but the minute you start talking to them, you realise that a good number of those people do not have that 'pleasing' personality. Any thoughts of wanting to get to know them have already timed out. Now think of someone you have had great conversations with. Your partner, your friends, etc., with whom you can discuss anything and everything, and you know their character and opinions add a lot to your talk and outlook on life. Some of these people might not have caught your eye when you first met them, but they surely are the ones you loved talking to and would want to continue being in touch with. Out of both of these categories, which one would you pick? Would you want someone who looks attractive but has no substance, or would you prefer someone who may not be as attractive but is a great human?

The choice here is a little too obvious, isn't it? Yes, our world depends on appearance, but it can only take you so far in life. Your looks may get you through some doors in life, but how you manage to stay inside that room depends on your personality. Even if you are attractive, it does not mean much if you are one-dimensional with nothing else to offer. Your beauty might as well be a waste.

For authenticity and realness in life, being true to your character and personality is much more critical. Today, the world is run by beauty industries, but think about it, can they really make you beautiful? No, they cannot. Because someone's beauty or ugliness has nothing to do with what they look like but instead has everything to do with what kind of a human being they are. Beauty takes a backseat then, and in fact, it might not even be the picture after initial meetings. In the end, personality matters because no matter how attractive someone is, they are not a painting for you to stare at. They are human beings, and humans have much more to offer than looks. Those individuals can be the other half of a great partnership if they become willing enough to change if that's even a desired and reachable option for them. Two people who have been together for a while grow older together simultaneously. You no longer get to date the guy in the picture when we met, and I find myself with whom I signed up to last.

CHAPTER 11

UNHAPPY WITH YOURSELF? CHANGE!

This qualifies as more than on a
need-to-know basis, thanks for the heads up!"

If you know something about you needs work, chances are that the people around you know it as well, but don't be alarmed by this fact. I do not mean it scarily, that everyone around you points at you and laughs secretively. Instead, it stands to be an example of how you are so self-aware. Identifying anything that's not right, or in a sense, "wrong," means you're halfway to fixing it. However, if you still do not realize or are oblivious to what needs improvement, that should truly scare you.

The whole idea of fixing yourself means that you are improving. In doing so, you understand who you are and how you can improve, and then act on becoming better. This takes a lot of courage and willpower. Let's look at it this way—your brain is your COO (Chief Operating Officer); it controls "every move you make and every breath you take." This is why you are also officially dead if your brain is dead. Nothing you do or think about gets by unless your brain approves it first. So, aside from first identifying and acknowledging what you want to improve about yourself, your brain also helps you decide whether you have the fortitude, willingness, desire, ability, etc., to carry out this undertaking. If the decision is to move forward, it goes to the action department, where things begin to happen. Again, your brain, and for some, a higher power or God of their understanding is always there to coach you alongside until you achieve your goal.

This whole process can be very inspiring and life-altering if you let it. As humans, we all have flaws that need fixing. We all have attributes with room for improvement. If you want to improve yourself, simply minimize what you don't like about yourself and do what you already do even better. Your brain might think you need emotional, mental, or physical improvement. If you need to be fitter, get up, exercise, and get in shape. Perhaps a change or a makeover is in order, so try to balance out your life. Work hard but pamper yourself. Massages can also significantly help your body; whenever I get one, my friends tell me that I look refreshed and relaxed. Yoga is also great for your mind, body, and soul. And I don't want to come across as a typical doctor, but a good diet and lots of water are good for the skin. Eat well because, yes, "you are what you eat."

Of course, you cannot change yourself if you do not assess yourself. To do so, I will recommend a little activity. Take a blank sheet of paper, and draw a vertical line down the middle of it. On one side, write 'ASSETS'; for the other column, give it the headline 'DEFECTS.' Now, think about yourself and keep adding points on both sides. It can be an asset for you that you are funny, but it might be a liability that you are shy. You might be fit and smart, but also moody, pessimistic, etc. Sit down and truly think about yourself. Keep adding qualities as and when you remember them.

And by the end, you know what you need to be more and what you need to engage in less.

But yes, knowing yourself is not enough. All your knowledge of yourself will be for naught if you do not act upon it. The difference between those who make it and those who don't all comes down to action. We all have the potential to achieve great things, yet not all of us have the grit to do it. Remember, one who wears the crown first needs to bear the crown. My mother often said, "God gave you so much, so why are you wasting it?" This question has always motivated me to do more. Instead of seeing our flaws as something to cry about, I have always seen them as ways of improving myself and proving it the world and to myself that we are what we make of ourselves. Do you want to be a better version of yourself? Do you want to be fitter? Happier? Calmer? More considerate? Adventurous, perhaps? You could want to be anything you want, but it can only be achieved if you work on it. The question is—how badly do you want to?

CHAPTER 12

EVERYONE LOVES BEING LIKED

"Wherever you go, there are people like us. People are waiting to like and be liked, and even to love if you can love."

Some might love you until you die, and some might just stay with you until you die.

QUICK-WITTED AND VERY WELL-LIKED, my Uncle Buddy was everyone's favorite. Of course, Buddy wasn't his real name, but that is what everyone had always called him. And honestly, the nickname suited him a lot as he was truly of everyone's "buddy." Whether a stranger or a relative, every single person who had ever known him. He was quite the opposite of my father. My father had always been the serious type, the one who was way too reserved to ever be outwardly funny. He was more of a business type, so it was no surprise that many people, especially those looking for a smile, preferred my uncle over my dad. Ironically, my dad was widely known as "Buddy" Breitweiser his entire life, and a tattoo which proves that. As a matter of fact, my brothers and I carried the nickname "Bud" for short all of our adolescents.

Almost all my cousins were close to me in age, which meant that our family get-togethers were always filled with fun. I still remember the numerous times Uncle Buddy would take us to a game, or to go crabbing off the piers in New York, or even up the block for ice cream. He did develop diabetes in his later years, which eventually was the cause of his death, but on numerous occasions, he would tell my aunt, "Patsy, get the kids some cake." What great times we had as cousins because of everyone's favorite Uncle Buddy! He was a truck driver who once came home with front-row tickets right behind the Met's dugout for a game against the Cincinnati Reds in 1970. Johnny Bench, my all-time favorite, even hit a homer that day!

To this day, I still think about Uncle Buddy from time to time, but I cannot help but compare him to my father. Yes, my father had garnered the utmost respect from everyone he met, but Uncle Buddy had made all of them laugh and smile. In life, you would have to decide if earning someone's respect or their love is more important to you, but I guess if you earn their love, you automatically have their respect. I have always said, "I wanna be the best friend to all my friends." "I'd Rather Be Nine People's Favorite Thing Than a Hundred People's Ninth Favorite Thing" is the title of a song from a Broadway Musical, but this one title tells you all you need to know. If you spread love and positive vibes to the ones around you, you are doing all you need to do.

SELF-CONSCIOUS IS TOO CONSCIOUS

"We can look good every day of our lives if we just tell ourselves we are good enough."

In my life, I have been fortunate enough to know some people whose outlook on life has been different than others. Of course, some change with time, and some might have gained a little weight or more wrinkles, but even if someone mentions things like this to them or points it out, it does not phase them much. Instead, they would come up with a way of downplaying it. "Oh, it's nothing much!" "C'est la vie!" "Can't count calories when you are too busy enjoying life!" Such an outlook on life is awe-inspiring, and I wish I could be that way. But sadly, I am not. I think being single and having never been married probably has something to do with it, but ultimately, the broader problem is that I am too self-conscious and unable to like myself just as I am.

Have you ever been to a hair salon and gone through the magazines they keep in a stack as you wait for your turn? These magazines, having perfect-looking people and their impeccable hair stylings, excite you because now you want to look this flawless as well. So, you excitedly point the photo to your barber and ask if you could look the same. And half-jokingly, they would say, "I can replicate the cut, but the face will be yours."

Most people have deep-seated insecurities about their appearance, and yes, the magazines and TV and everything in the glamour world does not help the case. A considerable part of the problem remains that you think that what you see in these magazines are the real beauty standards, not realizing that these photoshoots and models have a whole team of hair and makeup, not to mention the editing that is done on these photos. This causes you to compare yourself to unrealistic standards and set your own self up for failure. I am guilty of doing the same as well. But if you want to break out of this circle, you will have to realize that sooner or later, the reality of these unrealistic standards will have to be faced. We must be reasonable and remind ourselves that we can never be like them because this photo is unreal.

Look at the people in that photo in any other candid setting, and you will realize that not even they look like themselves. This is why it is essential to realize that we are who we are, and whosoever we are is enough. While grooming is vital, you do not have to be overtly conscious of your looks and cry over them. You are good enough the way you are, and even if you want to work on yourself, doing so will only be beneficial if you do it with a positive mind. You will only be better if you want to, for example, lose weight to be healthier, but if you want to go on crazy diets and starve yourself to attain a zero figure, it won't work. A counselor I knew once told me to keep telling myself that "I am worthy!" With this, what she wanted me to know that I am somebody, and that, in itself, was enough. Everyone is somebody, and everyone has something to offer to this world and something to feel good about themselves.

In my first book, I admitted to being a person in the long-term recovery of addictions. Before telling this to people, the fact of anyone knowing used to scare me. But today, it doesn't bother me one bit. I used to be scared of what people would say and how others would react, but today, I have learned to admit it and deal with it as confidently as possible. So much so that someone asked me what I did for a living in one of my AA meetings after hearing me talk. I told him I was a writer, and he replied, "That makes sense. I have heard you share before and thought you were a public speaker." Just his statement was enough to tell me how far I had come. From not facing it to facing it so confidently and working on improving it!

You might be one of the people who struggle with themselves, and it is okay, because, yes, it is a long process. To accept yourself, you must start by being comfortable with your brain. Being comfortable with yourself is the first step to being confident, or at the very least, being content with who you are. Accepting you for you and seeing it positively is very important. As we age, we realize that we are ever-growing. If you worry too much about your insecurities, you spend more time fixing the car than driving it."

CHAPTER 14

YOU CAN HANDLE THIS

*"Oh, that Barney Rubble...
what an actor"—1982 "Night Shift"*

If the entire world is the stage, then all of us are actors. Yes, we have already established that, but how well of an actor are you? Are you award-worthy? Of course, you are...when you are alone. You can act brilliantly when you are alone, just like me. I am a great actor on my own. If nobody is watching me, I can enact scenes from movies, play air guitar like Jimmy Page, lip sync to multiple songs, and put on a whole concert by myself. But all of it is when I am alone.

Without stage fright, all of us can be great actors, and in this scenario, people around us often create this stage fright. In real life, the role of acting is about being authentic and as natural as you can be. Then acting is being who you truly are in front of everyone. Being able to close your eyes to everything around you while keeping them open. In reality, there is no centerstage, camera lens, or audience waiting just for you. You also exist amongst all the other actors in the world, putting on a show simultaneously.

Yet, in my experience, the biggest problem arises when you are actually in the spotlight, where everyone is looking at you., This usually happens in the case of public speaking projects. Many people in this world are petrified of public speaking, but it is also true that whatever fears live in their heads are also created by their heads. The real problem is never the five minutes or the ten minutes, the actual time you stand in front of a group of people but rather the hours and days of overthinking what could happenin that short time at center stage.

If you know what you are speaking about and are well prepared, you will soon be one with the room. You just need to take a "leap of faith". Once that first sentence pours out, you'll be rolling smoothly like a train pulling away from the station. These people in the audience are usually just listening to you. If you think about it, "the public" is a bunch of strangers, and you usually only feel uncomfortable amongst them because you do not know them. Your fear dissolves as soon as you know them and see known faces in the crowd. A song by The Doors significantly explains it—

"People are strange…when you're a stranger".

This whole public speaking session, not to mention everything else, would be so easy if you already knew everyone and everyone knew you. You would not have to waste your time worrying about strange reactions, and you could depend on them a bit as you already knew them. Yes, it all sounds so easy, but we know reality does not work like that.

Public speaking can be a little scary, but there are multiple ways of overcoming these awkward moments. 1. Preparation and some preliminary exercises are great tools for dealing with emotional discomfort or uneasiness. Nothing can stand in your way if you are relaxed and ready to go. 2. Rehearse your presentation in front of a mirror or with a friend a few times. Rehearse, rehearse, rehearse, until you know everything by heart. 3. Mediate and calm yourself down. It is just a presentation, not the end of the world. I, too, literally pray every time I have to speak in public, and it does help me gain strength. I always say: "Dear God, don't let me bomb. I don't know if I can handle being booed off the stage. And if I do, help me to be better next time."

Some of these ways are usually bound to help you, and you will soon realise that it wasn't as big of a deal as you were making it out to be. You might have heard something advise you to imagine all the people sitting there in their underwear, but that doesn't work. What works in you is finally understanding that the ones listening to you are also people just like you, so whether you are speaking or conversing, know them or not, they are just regular people like you, and they are just here to listen to you. It isn't that big of a deal, I promise. You can handle this!

CHAPTER 15

WHAT FEARS?

*"If you're on guard, or on the lookout all the
time, you are mostly living in a form of fear"*

The word 'fear' comes to mind whenever we talk of phobias. Fear of spiders, fear of snakes, fear of heights, fear of confined places, etc.—all of these are phobias and legitimate ones. Any term that ends in "phobia" indicates that it is something that certain individuals in our world are truly, sincerely afraid of. But is this the only context in which we use 'fear'? If a phobia, such a severe condition, tells us that someone is fearful of something, should we then stop calling other, not-so-serious conditions, 'fears'? I think so because, in reality, a lot of things we count as fears are usually just concerns or worries. Which sounds more appropriate to the situation—"I am fearful of failing my test" or "I am concerned that I may fail this test"? Do you say, "I am fearful of losing my job," or do you think you are worried that you might lose your job? I think you know the answer, which proves my point that fear and concerns or worries are on different scales, and not letting your worries escalate to fear is the first step in dealing with them. Save the fearful word 'fear' for actual phobias.

In the previous chapter, we discussed the biggest fear people will ever face, fear of public speaking. I believe that is all in your head and your own making. I like to call it undue anxiety. In front of an audience, it's not what you're about to say but the time thinking about what you are planning to say. Then suddenly, you are being looked at by everyone in the place.

You know fear is a powerful emotion, and it has the capacity to tie you up in such a way that your growth stays forever hindered. It is true; pick a scenario, any scenario. There's a consideration for fear, or any level or variation of it, in any topic or situation. It doesn't matter which, because we humans tend to attach the word fear to every possible thing. Your scenario could be that you fearful of losing your job, getting more workload, or being forced into a higher tax bracket, earning more, etc. It could even be the fear of being rejected by your infatuation. You might have gotten your crush's number in total excitement, but now that you are supposed to text them, millions of fears crop up in your mind— What if they don't like how I text? What if they don't like my taste in music? What if they think I am boring? What if? What if? What if?

In all of these cases, you are letting fear rule your life. Richard Carlson said, "Don't sweat the small stuff," and he was right because if you let these worries and concerns run around for too long, they will continue growing and end up becoming fears and phobias. Maybe your crush truly was meant to be your soulmate and life partner, but you would never know because you let the concern of them not liking you enough convert itself into fear, and hence, you never even texted them in the first place.

Oscar Isaac said that "When it feels scary to jump, that is exactly when you jump, otherwise you end up staying in the same place your entire life!". Quite simply, it means that you'll never realize your full potential in life if you don't even try. If you let your concerns and worries turn into fears, you will remain stagnant, never achieving anything at all. Yes, if you never do anything at all, you will never fail, but remember that it also means that you will never succeed, which automatically means that you have failed.

We all have fears and concerns; it is quite natural to have them. Yet, letting them guide your entire existence and actions is not realistic. You shouldn't let your fear hinder your progress. You lose more by never trying than you do by actually failing. The world is filled with people who never achieve their dreams because they never allow themselves to take the leap. Do you want to be one of them? Let me ask you something: if not you, then who, and if not now, then when? Many people never reach greatness due to fear. Fear to take the risk that they may fail. Fear of losing their sense of security.

CONFIDENCE IS VERY BECOMING

"The confident one is unwavering.
Knows a direct path to everything.
The attention they get is about all they need."

As we have already established, being attractive has nothing to do with how you look, but rather everything to do with how you carry yourself. It depends on the kind of person you are; of course, your confidence is one of its major factors. The level of confidence that lies within you is a contributor to the attractiveness you showcase to the outside world.

Puzzlingly, an infectious display of Charisma can bring on goosebumps. It's almost embarrassing to be captivated by just one's way they handle themselves. Their indelible level of confidence and style need be their only ticket. And so, the good fortunes of their inner beauty affords them what many glamourous and prominent ones futilely strive to have.

Confidence, or self-confidence as it were, is a fantastic character (inner quality) trait and reflects in how others perceive you. If you have self-confidence, you are usually unafraid of the outcome. You possess the most profound understanding of humility. You are comfortable in your own skin and are not swayed by the actions of others. If you have self-confidence, you might even appear intimidating to others.

Yet know that true self-confidence differs from other bold character traits, like ego, pride, and arrogance. Self-confidence knows the importance of mindfully managing itself so that you don't run wild and turn narcissistic. Self-confidence, in its true sense, gives you a healthy level of self-esteem. Not to mention how much it changes your life on an everyday basis. For example, imagine you and a coworker (let's name him Jim) are both assigned to the same project. Both of you have given it your all to the project, and it truly is a 50-50 effort, yet when the boss comes in to praise the duo for it, it is Jim who gets more pats on his back and more claps. Why is that? Well, because he was more confident. In your meetings with the team, he was the one always pitching in ideas to everyone. He proposed statements, gave PPTs (PowerPoints), and took the lead. On the other hand, you worked on the project just as hard but were too self-conscious to speak much in the meetings. You were too shy to give presentations and inputs in front of the boss, giving everyone the impression that Jim was working harder than you. This is the difference self-confidence can make.

A person who displays a high level of confidence and is entirely sure of themselves is treated differently than those who are weaker and unsure of themselves.

Back in 1973, when Kiss (the band) was first starting out, they conducted auditions for a lead guitar player. As told by the band's founders Gene Simmons and Paul Stanley, they had gone through around 50 players when Ace Frehley, wearing two differently-colored sneakers walked in. He didn't acknowledge anyone, he just walked over to the amplifier everyone was using, plugged in his guitar, and started playing. And the rest was history! Self-confidence is all about the way you present yourself every minute of your life, whether you are doing something important or a mundane task. And one of the most prominent signs of self-confidence is being quick-witted. When you are not afraid of the words that come out, you are self-confident. And even though I believe confidence can be learned with practice, having a quick wit is innate in few. However, you can improve your level with practice and experience.

UPHOLDING INTEGRITY

One of our human survival skills is security.
Whether you're the giver, or the taker,
it would be foolish to discount the importance
of being responsible and having integrity.

When we usually talk of someone being attractive, a few qualities come with this title. We have already discussed that self-confidence is one, and now, I am only to tell you about the second-most important one—being responsible. Who isn't wowed by someone responsible? This one quality has the power to make you shine in the eyes of others. If you are responsible, you constantly display your integrity through actions. But know that integrity, though, is a quality that is earned.

When discussing family integrity, it is frequently the case that the first generation is more responsible than the others. Because they are usually the ones who start with nothing and end up building an entire life for themselves. Their children are already born into the life created by their parents or caretakers, meaning that they have a lot more than the generation before they did. Don't we see a similar case in celebrities and their kids? We know of many actors and singers who work hard to even get their first opportunity, and then we see their kids, who, with the power of the responsible life their parents built, get everything they want from the get-go.

But no matter who you are, whether the first generation or the one born to responsible parents, you need to work hard to become accountable for your own identity. In the beginning, you only have a name—a famous one or not. From there, you must formulate your identity and impression of others. This cannot be a one-time process; think of it as building a campaign over time, even a lifetime, and most certainly an honest one. But integrity can also be easily lost by becoming irresponsible, and in most cases, it isn't easy to regain, so work on it carefully and consciously. The more you "screw up," the more your integrity score goes down.

With friends, being responsible means they can count on you. With family, it denotes that you will take care of them and support their ups and downs. With society, it means you will be a responsible citizen. Being responsible can mean different things at different stages and in front of different audiences, yet the point remains that everything in life deserves a level of responsibility, and that is what makes you an attractive human being. Whether you are the one responsible or depending on someone else to be so, it would be foolish to discount the importance of having integrity. Being responsible is all about being in control of yourself.

There might be a lot of people in the world who are attracted to your face, money, or connections, but are those the ones you want around? In our true sense, we all want people who like us for who we are and are attracted to us for our actual qualities. If you are responsible, it becomes one of those qualities and makes you stand apart from everyone else. Being responsible means being enterprising, a doer, and driven by nature. You are the one who usually possesses great ethics, and that you can take care of yourself and others around you.

CHAPTER 18

SHOWING RESPECT

"The easiest way to gain respect is by showing respect."

Do you want to change something in yourself? Do you want to be a better version of yourself? Do you want to be appreciated and loved by everyone you meet? Your answer to all these questions might be a 'yes,' which is why you are reading this book. But before you try to find ways to achieve all of these and change yourself entirely for the world, let me halt your march. When the question comes down to how much respect and admiration the society around you showers on you, the answer to it comes from your actions and your deeds. Of course, if you do great things, make life-altering inventions, or are immensely talented, the world will notice you. It might even appreciate you to some extent. Yet know that if you are someone who doesn't treat someone else with respect, you will never have theirs, despite all your achievements on paper.

Human beings live with each other in the same circle, expecting a variety of things from the person next to them. One of them is respect. If you want to be a hit with the ones around you, start by being nice and kind. Nobody expects you to bend over backward for someone else, but know that not much love will be given to the heartless individual who isn't respectful to others. So much of this world operates interdependently, so it does pay to treat others how you want to be treated. Be mindful in all your affairs. Catch yourself, and always make it right. Think about how "I" would like to be received. What do I want to hear, or how do I want to be treated? Personally, I don't want more than I deserve or less, either. And certainly, without false pride. Not to be appeased or played. Betrayed or undermined. Is this not reasonable? I want that, and how I want that for you too.

Not just with the people around you, you also have to be truthful and respectful to your own self. You can never fully metamorphose unless you know and accept yourself. Understanding who you are puts you in the optimal position to become as great and 'best' as possible. Where change might be in order, begin this project that is you. Only then can you ever earn respect from the outside and the inside. Start your journey slowly and deliberately. This is not a path you can cross in a day but rather a walk you have to continue for as long as you live. It takes a lifetime, but the goal is always to find the best way to live and stick to it.

When the question comes to the 'my best' and 'respect,' know that these words do not mean being famous and earning a lot of money. Those factors can be on your bucket list, and it isn't necessarily wrong to aim for them in proportion. But ask yourself what your actual goal is. What does your heart and mind aim to achieve to be a good and respected human being? What are the steps that can be taken in climbing that hill? When you pause and concentrate on what your heart wants and not your greed, the hints will crop up on their own. You will know that the way to respect is always the way of honesty.

I have tried my best to be a respectful person. I have ensured that I treat everyone around me with the utmost respect and receive the same from them. I respect myself enough to stand up for myself, take what's mine, and never aim for something that belonged to someone else. There have been times when I wished I had done something differently. There were times when I wasn't my best self, but such moments have taught me to be better for the rest of the time. If I have not been honest with myself or those around me, I knew I needed to come clean and start afresh. It is the effort that you put into mending the wrongs that earn you respect. Respect yourself enough to tell yourself when you are wrong. And respect yourself enough to amend those wrongs. Put your best forth in everything you do. Respect yourself and be fair to yourself.

We're taught to let things go when others have wronged us. So our first instincts are to want to get even. Somehow, we think that evening the score reduces the pain. But, in reality, the tact we take is usually a regrettable one. I have often said that we all carry only our own conscience. And I can add to that by saying we all have a portable recorder in our heads to remind our conscience repeatedly how dumb our thoughts, and perhaps even our actions, were. Whether you do or don't believe in Karma, you don't have to be part of what might happen next. If you have completely let it go, no more action is required.

Adherence to all these principles are the building blocks for more-than-adequate self-esteem and self-respect. It's the conduit between our inner qualities and the way we treat others. If we have truly learned to respect ourselves, we can complete the cycle by showing the same respect to others. Give respect and gain it.

UNSELFISH, BUT UNAPOLOGETICALLY ME.

"Take what's yours and leave the rest.
There should be enough for others if
you are fair about your share."

Kindness, politeness, and everything that falls between, under, or around these two are usually thought to be the epitome of being a good human being. We have always been taught to be the same, but nobody has ever defined to what extent we should follow it. Selflessness is a good trait when you think of it in terms of helping others and adding something precious to our world, but is it right to be selfless at the cost of your senses and sanity?

"I am me"—I have used this phrase to justify many of my life actions. I have used it whenever someone disregarded my thoughts or wanted something of me that I couldn't give. I have used it apologetically because, with this one phrase, I am saying that I am who I am and everything I am created to be. I can only be me and make the most out of what was given to me, in whatever case.

I know selflessness has been taught to us since we were young, and we were all taught to never be selfish. It was a bad, bad thing to be selfish, but think about it, is it really? I think being a little selfish is okay. Because it is the selfishness that wills you to put your needs above others in a self-preserving way. If you act too selfless and give away everything anyone needs, you would be everyone's favorite piñata, and everyone would take advantage of you. So, it is not that selfish to be a little selfish.

If you work hard and buy yourself a few luxury things, are you selfish if you don't want to share them with the rest of the world? What truly would be selfish and ugly is when you'd disrespect those things. When I was a young boy, I had a few odds jobs—paper routes, mowing lawns, shoveling snow, etc. All of these were small jobs but were enough for me to work hard and save up enough for a green Schwinn Varsity 10 speed. It was one of the best moments of my life because I was so proud of myself and the bike I had paid for with my own money. In fact, I was so proud that I became protective of my bike. I didn't want just anybody riding it and resulting in scratches. And all of my friends already had a bike anyway, so I didn't feel that bad saying no. There were adults around me telling me that I should share, but honestly, I didn't want to because I knew my friends, and I was sure they'd end up harming my bike. Even if they say sorry in the end, what good would it be if my new bike was already beat up? Yes, I was being a little selfish, but it was to protect myself and my investment.

And being selfish and unapologetic can be a good thing because these traits will help you reach your goals. Socrates advised two things: care for yourself and know yourself. He and many other great minds like me understood the importance of being a little selfish because that meant taking care of yourself. If you do not take care of yourself and offer yourself up for someone to take advantage of, you will never reach the goals you are supposed to reach.

Mind you, there still is a difference between true selfishness and having preservation instincts. If you put yourself first without letting anyone else take advantage of you, that is good selfishness. But it is not a good thing if you only put yourself first, even at the expense of others. You should preserve yourself, but never at the cost of others. That is the actual difference between the two concepts. So, be a little selfish, just enough to ensure that nobody else can use you, but never do the same to anyone else.

CHAPTER 20

EXPECT LITTLE.
LET DOWN LESS EXPECTATIONS

*"If I put a lot of faith in most people,
I find that they don't listen well. And if they
heard me, then they just don't respect me."*

Shakespeare once said that expectation is the root of all heartache, and he wasn't wrong. Humans have many character flaws, and one of the biggest among them is expectations. I am sure many of you also have been a victim of this evil thing; if you have, don't worry. I am in the same boat as you. Expectations always seem to cause me the most trouble, and I am sure the same can also be applied to you. Almost 80% of the people you meet in your life are not true to their intentions. Most of them do not even have any intentions, but not even 1% of them will tell this directly to your face. The truth is that this gets to me because I, too, am sometimes weak, as to not be afraid to say what I am thinking. That is my part in this, and I must recognize and continue to live with the outcome or change my attitude.

How many times have you had people promise to do something for you, yet they never do it? Many of them even try to emotionally manipulate you, and I am sure you have already heard all of these dialogues—"I am not like that at all." "My word and integrity rank too high for me to be disloyal to you." "I would never do this to you."

You might have even heard bigger and better lies, and for a lot of them, you might have even wanted to yell because you got so fed up with these deceptions. You'd try to give them many chances to stand up to the expectations, but after repeated failures, you'd get so frustrated that the only solution is to cut them off and be thankful. Has this never happened to you?

Wouldn't life be so much easier if people did what they said they would? Wouldn't everything be better if people didn't give you false expectations if they do not want to stand true to them? It will save all of us from such unnecessary drama, wouldn't it? But for some reason, humans like to complicate things, so they end up creating expectations and then end up disappointed. It would be realistic to think that if someone does this to you, they are disrespecting you. And not just that, but they are also disrespecting themselves. It's as simple as that.

Maybe it is not as important to them as it is to you, but this is where your selfishness needs to kick in. After you realise that they have spoiled the integrity of your relationship, you need to preserve yourself, not the relationship. It is a very hard thing to do. I do not deny that, but it is what needs to be done. This bitter truth will hurt you in a small way, but it will be beneficial to you in the long run.

I have devised a way to help you deal with such situations a little better. First, rate the person who has created the expectation and then rate the priority of that expectation. How important is this task to you, and how disappointed would you be if it was not fulfilled? Now, come back to the person. How much do you know about them? How much do you trust them? Do you have any history with them, or are they someone important to you? Keeping all of these things in mind, lower your expectation level. If you are expecting something incredible from someone you have only known for a while, then chances are that you are setting yourself up for failure. They may surprise you and actually fulfill those expectations, but know that it is way better to be surprised than to be disappointed.

It is okay for you to be a little pessimistic in certain situations. This should only be in viable, and rare, at most, circumstances in such cases where you are preserving yourself (but not at the expense of others). See the pattern of your expectations, and if you have been let down a lot of times, it is finally time for you to be pessimistic. You will need to put your foot down to preserve yourself. The ones around might even think that you are setting a boundary, which would be correct. You will need to understand where you come first and definitely over others. Draw the line, especially in difficult and tricky situations. Block them out. It is better to be a blocker than a griever.

Expectations don't just occur involving other people. Have you ever made plans around the weather? One way to minimize your exposure to "a let" down based on expectations might not be to book a trip to Disney in August during their rainy season. Here you can take a little credit for using common sense and a little logic by working with the weatherman.

Has this ever happened to you? You're at a traffic light that just turns green, but you are many cars back. You don't expect to make it in this batch, but certainly, expect to make it with the next one. Then when you are just about to go, you hear sirens, and everyone stops. Oh NO, not fire engines! … "I'm never going to get to where I am going." These things happen. So leave a little cushion for life's moments.

CHAPTER 21

POPULARITY CONTEST

*"It can be a cruel, cruel world, but God
has us all worked into his equation."*

I REMEMBER IT WAS 1972 BECAUSE Crocodile Rock by Elton John was a big hit on the radio. As a big fan, music has constantly reminded me of all the different times of my life. It was sometime in "72" that Michael S. from around the block said, "I'm not your spare tire." I still remember him saying it to me like it was yesterday. His statement meant I couldn't just come by to play with him when no one else was around. I have also heard someone use "flat leaver," meaning you cannot dump them when others show up. Both are hurtful situations, and yet both are correct emotions to have.

In a similar scenario, I can now say my dad was very clever when he bought me a basketball in grammar school. I was not very tall, but tall enough to be picked to play and be the one with the ball. I remember playing "ball" in the schoolyard as a kid. We all played baseball, football, basketball, stickball, and street hockey… and I played them all. And if you brought the ball, you got to play regardless of how good you were.

Because of my size, I was probably always the last one picked, but I always got to play a crucial figure in every game as the kid with the ball.

We are the main character in our lives, so we only focus on ourselves, but the same can be applied to everyone else. You might think someone you bumped into once on a bus has no significance, but they might feel the same about you. All of us are someone, so we deserve to be treated with some respect. We already know these things, yet we are guilty of forgetting them at times, especially when we are often selfish.

This can be seen a lot more in people who are "popular," whether you are popular worldwide, in your nation, town, school, etc.

Popularity is like winning an award in a world obsessed with being on top. Being popular means that everyone wants you, and you can always have your pick. Popular means you're always part of anything you choose. You make every team, and you're presumably brilliant. Some people have the good fortune to step into popularity. A parent or older brother or sister who preceded them may have paved the way or has even made things more difficult.

You may have your picks on things or even people, but it does not give you the right to treat someone in a worse way. If you are picking someone, know that they are also picking you back and can drop you as quickly as you dropped them. Nobody is your spare tire, especially people. If you treat them as such, chances are they will realise the expectations they have set will never be fulfilled, and they will roll away from you. And they will no longer treat you with the respect or admiration you are used to. Humans are to be treated like the people they are and not as a temporary fix to your immediate desires. If you do not want to engage someone, the most honourable thing is to let them know. If you would not like it done to you, why would you be willing to put someone else through it?

CHAPTER 22

THERE'S ALWAYS A MOTIVE

What is truly and deeply behind your thinking?
Is it what drives you? What you're in it for?

One way of realising how others should be treated is knowing how you should treat your self. So often, how we treat others stems from our feelings or our insecurities. And we can only do away with such insecurities when we start being kind to ourselves and accepting ourselves. It all seems like such hard work, but being ignorant and taking it out on others only buries us even more. If you want to achieve self-realization, it has to begin with self-compassion.

The need of the hour is to stay attuned to yourself and to realize who you are. If you know it, the entire process of becoming a better human becomes more effortless. Realise who you are and what your liabilities are, as we discussed in a previous chapter. But know that these liabilities will only stay as 'liabilities' if you let them be. It is in your power to turn those liabilities into assets without judging yourself too harshly or blaming yourself for having them in the first place. Just because you need some work does not mean you are unworthy or different from others; keep this in mind at all times, as it is a vital reminder required at every step. You are a human being, and no human being is ever perfect. With this realisation, you can treat yourself better.

You must learn to be good to yourself and show yourself some self-compassion. You might have heard the phrase "treat others how you want to be treated," but how about you start this with yourself? How about you treat yourself the same way you treat others? It sounds straightforward, right? That is because it is, at least when you get into the habit of it. Learn to forgive yourself when you make a mistake. Don't judge your appearance so critically. We all have shortcomings in one way or another, so go easy on yourself if you don't always hit your mark. All of this will ultimately contribute to improving your self-esteem. As we discussed, some people might call you "selfish" for this, but again, there is nothing wrong with being a little selfish. The selfishness here makes you give equally to yourself.

Let me tell you a story: One night while watching TV, I saw a commercial of a young child who only had one shoe. She was wearing a pink dress and standing on a dirt road in some third-world country. Seeing her state saddened me and caused me to call that NGO (Non-Government Organization) and donate. That night was a little over 20 years ago, and on the same night, I ended up sponsoring two kids. Just doing that felt so good, just the very fact that I was able to do that. After that, I added two more kids under my sponsorship every time I saw a commercial highlighting the poor state of needy children worldwide. After six years, I had around 42 kids; I would get mail from them daily, sharing their drawings, photos, and letters. They would write to me—"This is my donkey." "This is my goat." "This is my little brother." Seeing their art brought tears to my eyes, but there were times when I looked at myself and wondered if I was being selfish. I thought I was only doing this to make myself happy, to feel better about myself. I thought I was only doing it for myself. But people around me would tell me that I was feeding, clothing, and educating kids who couldn't afford to do it for themselves. They told me that I was not selfish, and even if I was, a little selfishness was okay.

"What drives me to achieve what I want to achieve?" This question remains important and is relevant to every single thing you do. We all make goals for ourselves, and these goals motivate us to do the things we do and eventually achieve them. Whatever these goals or the reason for achieving them, the bottom line is about what they motivate you to do. You might do a few good deeds because you want to be a better person, but this motivation doesn't harm or taint your work. You are human, and that will always be how you think. It's okay. But the main focus is never your motive but your deed.

BUSINESS SALES AND SALESMANSHIP

CHAPTER 23

GETTING NOTICED

*"If you want to get someone's attention,
rise at every opportunity, always, and you may
have a fan who's already seen your work."*

I don't know when the thought of working continuously brewed in me, but if I had to pin it down to an event, it would be my first paper route as a young boy. My route consisted of four houses assigned to me by Mrs. Ammerman, but all four were in different corners of the town, which nobody wanted. Who the heck would want a four-housed paper route? Well, your answer would be a gullible eight or nine-year-old like me. Each delivery earned me 0.35c/week; in the end, I would have $1.40/week. These customers had been "house accounts," so they were billed monthly, so I never got any chance to collect the tip that might have come with cash. But this one odd route soon earned me bigger and more profitable routes.

Soon I was doing all kinds of odd jobs in the neighborhood. At 13, I was washing pots and pans at the Landmark II banquet facility, and next, I peeled potatoes at a gourmet deli. When that shop closed, the owner kept only me and one older woman to work at a liquor store he had newly started. When kids from high school were drinking beer in paper bags in the park across the street, I was mopping the floors, wishing I, too, could join them. But all my hard work paid off when I bought a 1965 Shelby Mustang at 16.

But things weren't always this great and inspiring. If you have read my first book, "I Didn't Ask to be Me," you know I had a problem with alcohol and substance abuse. As part of my treatment program, I was urged to get a job, regardless of the pay or the interest in the position. So, I took a job at TJ Maxx. It paid minimum wage and was one of the worst jobs I have ever had, but it was needed to teach me humility. Even the store manager who hired me was utterly baffled by my application. "Why do you want this job so badly"? he asked. This wasn't the first time someone asked me as I had taken various minimum wage jobs before where I was grossly overqualified for the position. Even before I could answer him, he said, "I get it. You're with the show. You're the "Undercover Boss." It took me a while to convince him I wasn't, but I soon started my professional journey there. I began in the jewelry department but was quickly promoted to the department manager of other parts of the store. My gig at that place lasted 16 months, and I finally quit with a degree in humility.

But while I worked the jewelry counter, I noticed some older ladies were regulars and would come in weekly. There were a lot of them, and they would always want to try on earrings, creating a ruckus. They were too excited to be tamed on this particular day, though I tried my best. But apart from the usuals, I could see that there was also a neatly-dressed gentleman from the corner of my eye, presumably waiting his turn. I tried to get the ladies to line up and behave, but when I couldn't, I stopped and said, "Sir, you are next if these women don't mind." The ladies were quiet and didn't want to give him the way, but thankfully for them, he said it was okay and the ladies could go first. When the dust settled, and he was the only one left, he told me that he had just retired from Porsche USA as Service Manager and wanted to offer me a job. "I've been watching you for a while, and I want to hire you," he said. "What would I be doing?" I inquired, to which he replied, "I don't know, but I like your style, so I'll find something for you." I gave him my number but never got the call.

The point of these stories remains that you never know who is watching you, whether it is your boss, a stranger, a future boss, or even the God of your understanding. So, it behooves you to always do your best. If you do your best at everything and try to compete with yourself to become better, the universe, sooner or later, will see you and recognize you. You will be rewarded for your hard work, no matter in what way, so always give it your all. Even if you don't want to do it for the person watching, do it for yourself because you are aware and improving, and that is all that matters. Looking back, are you able to recount all the jobs and chores you had to endure that you thought you'd never finish but made it through feeling accomplished?

CHAPTER 24

SCORING GOALS—NOT THE BIG SCORE

*With one great victory, you are the winningest for a
day. You don't wear your crown until you try again.
And so tomorrow, you'll only be in the books.*

Every time you hear a success story, it is the briefest version. Someone did this, won over the whole world, and made a name for themselves. Everything in such stories is all about grand adventures and big wins, but if you are living such a story, you know that the tale should instead be about the smaller wins that keep stacking on each other, ultimately giving you the grand stature. So, stop reading this book if you are looking forward to me pitching the sky to you. I won't tell you to randomly decide to run a 20 km marathon and win it the next day. That may sound like a great story to narrate in retrospect; the truth, does not work like that. The reality is about counting every single win, no matter how small.

In life, scoring goals is more about minor victories, whether accomplishments or milestone wins. Life, unlike what you have been told, is not necessarily about achieving a grand "set" goal but possibly about stringing together, enough wins to be a success in the big picture.

As a businessman, would you prefer one big contract or a smaller one every day? An argument could be made for both, but in this illustration, "the pennies add up to dollars." Think of it in terms of baseball. Watching the game, you love seeing home runs being hit, but if you were the team's manager, you would want the team to execute a "small ball" style of play with better odds of winning. Even if you watch as a fan, the same notion applies. If you were someone who'd turn their TV on just for the finals and watch an exciting game, you would want to see the players running the bases and many scoring frenzies. However, if you were a dedicated fan who has never missed a single game in the season, you probably wouldn't care as long as your team is victorious. So I ask you, "Do you want to witness a slugfest or a parade in October?"

The same applies to the way our life. The outside world may only count you as a hero if you achieve one great big thing. You could be Miss Universe or have a megahit hit at the box office or anything in between, but to you, the one living the life, it is more than just one big goal. In 1977, Styx, the rock band's song "Miss America," couldn't be more exacting of the pageant winner's ordeal.

If you have suffered or have ever known someone who has suffered from an addiction, then you know their goal is always getting through today. The strategy is always "one day at a time." The goal is to string together every single day to make a whole life addiction-free. Your goals can be small—completing a project with pride, winning a particular match, writing one page, studying one chapter, etc. The size of the goal does not matter, but its presence does. You have a goal for today and you will work on it today.

And it is only by thinking small that you can ever get too big. You cannot cover that entire 20 km of the marathon in one single step. You need to take smaller, shorter steps, but it does not mean that every single one of those steps does not count. You know they do. So, think small, do small, and little do you know that you will cover the marathon one day. My sister was a competitive swimmer and is a formidably-ranked marathon runner. She runs every day and increases the miles of her runs as the day of the race grows nearer. This small thinking will make you think big and lofty, making you move deliberately. The goal is to eventually reach your goals most successfully in due time. Make a solid commitment to yourself and your goals because every single one counts. You won't have to say, "I hope that someday…." But more like, "Today I am going to…."

CHAPTER 25

BUSINESS PLANS, ONLY BUT WITH LIFE

"I am one of those who even have to
plan to make a daily list."

When preaching about excelling in professional lives, the world claims many personal life lessons we can inculcate into our professional lives—forexample, being kind, staying steadfast and hardworking, giving everything our best, etc. Likewise, we can incorporate many qualities to create a successful career path for ourselves. Yet, the one thing we have overlooked is what our professional life can teach our personal one.

No business in the world can operate and succeed without a business plan. Such a plan is more than necessary to keep the business's operations on track and crosscheck whether what is being done matches the expectations with which the business was started. In theory and even in practicality, it seems like a vital tool; it can become even more important if we can tweak it to fit our personal lives.[A34]

If a business can have a plan to keep it on track, why can't life? Like a business, our life has various goals and hopes we aim to achieve. Not to mention how we work so hard to make them a reality. If such time, effort, and motivation are being invested in our life, won't it be in our best interest to track our progress? Doing so will allow us to ensure that our goals and our actions align as much as possible, giving a green signal to all our efforts.

As we discussed in the previous chapter, our life is built on goals, no matter how laborious or insignificant they may seem. These long-term or short-term goals add value to our lives and will us to work towards them, even giving us a purpose for existing. Presenting such great importance, it would be wise for us to improve and excel as human beings, to track these goals in our "life plans."

I have always been someone who has had a plan for myself. For as long as I can remember, I have woken up every morning knowing what I wanted to accomplish in the day, month, and even vague goals I wanted to touch within the year. I put together a new list for tomorrow every night to remain responsible and structured. President and 5 Star General Eisenhower's Matrix is a method to categorise and prioritise jobs by their urgency and importance. It is formed of four quadrants: Do, Decide, Delegate, and Delete. That's me! Usually, when the conversation comes to such life plans, we see the market today filled to the brim with unique stationery, binders, diaries, etc., all present and ready to help you keep track of things. They are a great way to start, especially when you are a beginner looking for a little organization, but know that actual life plans start way above any of these notebooks and fancy handwriting.

Just noting down things you want to do does not encompass all of what life plans should be; life plans, in my definition, stand to be greater than that. They do not just work to keep you on track regarding superficial goals, and they are an open platform that allows you to self-analyze and improve yourself. They are more of a worksheet for your evaluation, enabling you to monitor your progress and see how far you have come. Thus, what you add to your life plan also becomes just as important as a life plan in itself.

This book will help make you aware of both. By the time you are done writing it (your plan), you are to know which direction you want to explore in your life and how you want to go about it. You will be sure of what goals you have to set for yourself, whether vague or flexible, allowing you to alter them as per the situation. Or they are to be placed in concrete, pushing you to achieve them, no matter what But everyone is different. The details of the life plan surely will change with each individual, yet it is its presence and importance that I want to drill into your mind.

Come up with a few easy daily goals for yourself. Just 3-5 are enough to start you off. You can choose things like exercising, drinking a set amount of water every day, reading what stimulates you, etc. From this point onward till the end of the book, pay attention to the goals you have set. Learn the lessons this book teaches you, apply them wherever you can, and go after these goals you have listed. At the end of the book, come back to these goals and see if you have achieved them.

And if you ever waver, know that the most significant power to achieve these goals is within you. In an AA meeting, I learned the key to doing anything at all—desire. It stands to be a simple word, yet it holds the power to change your life. Do you desire to become better? Do you want to improve yourself? Do you want to achieve your goal? It presents itself as the first question to be tackled and the ultimate answer. It is the ultimate weapon; you must make up your mind to follow through.

CHAPTER 26

THIS MEANS A LOT TO ME (MOTIVATED AND PRIDEFUL)

*"Signing, stamping, or engraving your name
says pride and even responsibility.
Stand behind your work, not in front of it."*

Tommy and I have been friends for years, and as you remember, he was one of the guys who took me out to celebrate my 18th birthday (Chapter 3). In this years-long friendship, he and I have passed through multiple stages of our lives. One such stage was when Tommy worked on the floor in his father's steel company, and I worked inside an air-conditioned office. Since his job involved a good amount of manual work, he would constantly be tired by the end of the day. I could witness the exhaustion on his face whenever we'd catch up after work. But every time I answered his 'I am tired' with 'Me too,' he would be surprised. "How could you be tired?" he'd ask me; "all you do is sit on a chair the whole day!"

Hearing such words at the beginning of my career, to say the least, did not indite a great feeling in me; I had worked hard at my job the entire day, only to be told that my mental exhaustion did not amount to much. In the initial stages, such remarks hurt me and even demotivated me. Why would I want to work hard if the hard work was not even counted? Yet I persevered through all the negative comments and feedback, whether they were meant seriously or in a dig. I told myself that if I were to prove such comments wrong, I would have to show it, not just say it.

In life, there will be multiple occasions where you might be in a similar frame of mind. The pressure and the negativity need not be from an external factor; you could create it yourself. For example, someone else might tell you that your work isn't essential, or your brain might nag you that you aren't doing well. In such situations, the first step is the most vital—rejecting such ideas. You mustn't let your brain process and accept such claims. Instead, you are to tell yourself that the fate of the entire planet depends on the task at your hand. This is why you must treat it respectfully and complete it with utmost sincerity.

"How important is it to you that you finish your task with as much effort as you can afford?"—ask yourself this question repeatedly. If the answer is "very," know that you are motivated, mindful of what you do, and take pride in the tasks that touch your hands. But if the answer falls under "to some extent" or "not much," use it as a wake-up call. The tasks you complete and how you complete them are of utmost importance. For example, if you are assigned to write an essay of 5000 words, you should write all 5000 words and soak up the information present. But just writing those 5000 words is not enough. If you do so by copying them straight from the internet or from a friend's paper, it was merely a valueless exercise.

Your work and the effort put into it counts the most. Your motivation, goals, life plans, and everything in between hinge on it. So, be thorough with your work. Be devoted relentlessly. But most of all, be proud of every single thing you do. Such emotions, sadly, cannot be faked, which is why you must truly love the projects you take on. If you force yourself to perform a task, the results gained at the end can never match what you could have achieved while motivated.

But as humans, it is natural not to always feel 100%. Sometimes we want to give up or take a break, or even have valid reasons preventing us from giving it our all. The task, at such moments, becomes owning where you are and giving the situation as much as possible. Sometimes 80% can be better than an imaginary 100%. As the famous saying goes, "Done is better than perfect." I, too, have faced such situations various times. As a writer, a mental block can prevent you from giving it your all. The key to escaping any such situation, however, remains the same—push through until you get past it. For example, if I find myself putting off writing a book, I commission an artist to design its cover, even before I have started it. Such an act solidifies the presence of the task and forces me to write so my money does not go to waste. You might have heard some people do the same in their fitness journey—they keep clothes of their desired size and will work hard to fit into them, using that piece of cloth as their motivation.

You can derive this motivation to push through anything in life. It can be a promise of the future, a supporter who believes in you, or you yourself. At the end of the day, the point is to do the best you can with full faith. This has been my mantra throughout my life and has always been reflected in my work. When Tommy, years later, took over his father's business and started working more behind a desk than in a plant, he realized what I had said was right. He realized that work could be of different kinds, and one does not necessarily claim superiority over other. As long as you work with motivation and pride at what you have taken up, all the success is yours to claim.

FROM MY EXPERIENCE

"I believe there is only one definitive way to gain experience in anything. It's having been witness to something."

Experience—Rarely are things in life as precious as what it stands to be. Experience can shape us in ways unknown before that particular incident. "I saw," "I heard," "I smelled," and "I felt"—all these and much more have a way of giving us experiences that turn into life lessons and teaching. They motivate us to be a changed version of ourselves; if we are strong enough, it will be for the better. My experiences have always been great teachers to me, substantiating myself with new-found knowledge or cementing solid beliefs. And the same stands to be the truth for all of humanity. Our experiences, whether collective or individual, have shaped our history, knowledge, and understanding of life. Why else would we know factual truths like the temperature at which water boils or freezes, the gases we inhale and exhale, how the planet revolves around the sun, etc.?

When the conversation comes to experiences, it is a common belief that only the positive ones are to be remembered and looked fondly upon. This is the biggest lie we can tell ourselves and the people around us. The reality stands to be the exact opposite. Our mistakes, unfortunate incidents, mishappenings, etc., teach us much more. It teaches us what we can do better the next time and how to improve. If we do not experience negative experiences, we will never be willing to work and improve ourselves. Experiences help you understand yourself and the ones around you. They teach you what you like and don't like; whom you like and don't like; what works for you and what doesn't. It teaches you about yourself and humanity as a whole.

Yet, experiences can be a mystery; they can differ from person to person, and so can their outcome. If I were to leave two brothers in the Amazon Forest, would the experience for both of them be the same? A similarity in them might be noticed, yet an exact copy of each other they won't be. Perhaps one of the brothers is mentally and physically strong, quick, and persistent, able to handle the challenges the forest throws his way. But, on the other hand, the second brother could be of the weaker valor, unable to handle the pressures of the place. It is possible that one brother comes out of the jungle with an entirely new outlook on life, and the other one is scarred and suffers PTSD by the time he comes out, if he even comes out. In such a way, experiences, though a replica at the starting point, can be completely different by the end of them. This also proves that experiences, a vital part of making up life, are what you make of them. They can only teach you if you are willing to learn.

I have a younger brother Chris with whom I worked on several occasions over the years. I got to observe him and drew much from his ways. It's fair to say that he taught me a lot about business that extends to My everyday living. He's always reserved and never misspeaks. Calm and collected, and always very calculated. When I started writing this book, he would provide me valuable feedback, but being as stubborn as I was in my ways, I wasn't ready to accept his criticism. I was sure of my content and presentation, based on my experience, and thought of it to be superior knowledge. It was when I was writing this chapter that I realized how wrong I had been. I can't help but remember how tough he was on my writing for work. My "call" reports and emails had to be grammatically and punctually correct. I abbreviated everything. So, when I would get them back to redo, I would always respond with."you know what I'm saying—what's the big deal"? And he may have replied with: "It is a big deal; that's not how we write."

If life presents us with experiences of our own to learn from, who is to say our knowledge should stay limited to them? My experiences can teach me something, but if I allow myself, I can also learn from someone else's experiences. Of course, the lessons I take away from it might be different than what they conclude, but it would be unwise to close yourself off from learning, no matter whose experience it is through. In the end, after considering my brother's suggestions with an open mind, I realized his input was incredibly helpful to me in various places. Now that I have realized it, I am glad to have my brother and my friends as people around me, the people whose experience has taught me so much. I am sure that you, too, are surrounded by people you love and value—your family, friends, coworkers, etc. All of them are teachers for you and present you with an opportunity to learn. Consider their life and their experiences as an open book. Soak them in; learn something from them, and they will surely learn something from you.

CHAPTER 28

GETTING INTO YOUR SHOES—VALIDATION

"... You be me for a while,
And I'll be you."—The Replacements.

We are the protagonists of our lives, as we should be. We know that we are the main character, but we should not fail to remember that the people around us are our supporting characters or even more. Not to mention that they are the central figure in their own life as well, offering their own experiences and teachings to the world. No two people are the same, and no two experiences are exactly the same. Yet, we often forget to consider someone else in the spotlight we grant ourselves.

"Put yourself in my shoes"—all of us have heard or said this phrase once. With this, we are ultimately asking the other person to understand us and the world we come from. We ask them to get involved in our life and universe, not as a side character but as the protagonist. We ask them to understand who we are and why we have the characteristics we do. Finally, we ask them to stand in our place, allowing them to look at things from our perspective.

But what is the ultimate motive for doing so? What need would we have to take on the burden of someone else's viewpoint? Well, the answer is ingrained in the concept of empathy and validation. If we know what someone has experienced and dealt with, we can learn from them and understand their struggles. For example, for someone with a learning disability, writing down the alphabet would be a much different task. If we knew this, we would see the work they would have put in to get the results. To understand empathy and validation of this showcase, we must consider putting ourselves in someone else's shoes.

Empathy allows us to understand how others feel, aiding us with the proper response to validate them and their feelings. These skills go hand in hand with understanding, accepting, and appreciating someone and their struggles. Both are also vital in creating meaningful connections. It is no surprise that human beings are meant to live as a group, a society formed by creating towns, cities, states, nations, etc. All the people in a community depend on each other for survival and existence. This proves that understanding others and recognizing their feelings is the key to forming better and healthier relationships, as well as creating a space for a peaceful and accepting environment for everyone involved. As humans, we all require validation and empathy at one time; it makes us feel seen and heard and presents us with the belief that we are not alone.

It being such an essential factor in life ensures that all of us should know it and know how to implement it. Here are a few do's and don'ts you can follow:

DO

- Be conscious and accepting of people.
- Become curious about the changes in the behavior of people around you, and look for signs for help.
- Focus on the similarities than the differences. The people in the world have more in common than the differences we use to stand against each other. Use these similarities to build connections.

- Allow yourself to think from someone else's perspective. For example, if you are in a fight with a friend, try to understand their viewpoint instead of just trying to win the argument.

DON'T
- Be close-minded and ignorant. Open your ears and listen. You can only empathize and validate someone if you listen and understand their experiences. If you don't, you will remain ignorant.
- Downplay what someone feels. You may not feel the same way or even understand their reaction, but try putting yourself in their shoes. Recognize what someone else feels is valid.
- Invalidate the experience by stating that it could be worse. "At least it is not…", "It could be worse…" and other statements are counterproductive.
- Being defensive of the situation and offering unsolicited advice, does way more harm than good.

Jon, a guy who works at a retail store in Cartersville, Georgia, said validation was a big part of his position—validatingothers. Validation means acknowledging another person's emotions, thoughts, experiences, values, and beliefs. Validation isn't about agreeing, placating, or fixing the other person, trying to get someone to change or repeating back what the other person has said. Validation, just like empathy,

Using validation as a dialectical behavior therapy (DBT) skill communicates to the other person. Since DBT is all about managing negative emotions and learning how to change negative ones into positives, validation is a fantastic tool here. "You are important. Our relationship matters."

When validating others, we are not there to give advice. We merely accept how the other person feels and show empathy regarding what they are going through. So, it's a good idea to be a good listener. Siting a similar situation in your life lets the other person know "it happens to everyone." That creates a comfortable feeling which is precisely our purpose. Also, sharing similar experiences support the relevance of the situation, which is also comforting.

Jon also states that someone's emotions are evident in how they act, but he insists on listening to get to the problem area that needs solving. Make the customer happy. And sometimes, he must give them what they want plus something more to make them feel good about the situation they came to the customer service area for in the first place. But some must win out no matter what.

CHAPTER 29

THE POWER OF REMEMBERING

"If you really want to impress someone,
remember everything."

You have been reading the book I have written for the last few chapters, but do you know who I am? Do you remember my name, or do you need to flip back to the cover to remember it? Is it just my last name you remember, or do you know the first one as well? If you remember all of this without hints or cheating, thank you for making me feel special.

The belief of trivialities are not adding up to our substance has been a popular one in the recent past. Many believe that the little information we carry does not matter so much to our character. What our name is, our age, birth date, what fruit we like the most, what is our favorite drink, etc., do not amount to much, but that is not the entire truth. These trivialities end up piling up and creating our character, no matter howsoever small their addition is, which is why all of them matter, and the ones who remember them matter even more.

Do you know my middle name? Do you know my partner's name? My parents' birthday? The answer to these questions might be factual and available to most, yet the ones who remember it won't just be ordinary people. If someone were to know the answer to these questions, they would not be a mere acquaintance or friend. Instead, they would probably be one of my closest friends who know of these truths,and have also experienced them with me. Such an example proves the importance of remembering what others call trivialities.

Memory is one of our greatest assets. It helps us remember the things most important to us, which is why someone remembering information about us by heart showcases their love for us. Anyone can know my birthday, but only the near and dear ones would know how I like my coffee. And perhaps meet me for coffee on January 30th. If they are honoring me by adding information about me to their memory, it tells me they have paid attention.

But omitting something from memory does not necessarily translate into a lack of care. There can be instances of poor memory or things just slipping from our minds. The focusremains on the want to remember something because you appreciate someone. There are people in the world with a photographic memory who might remember how you ordered your coffee or which fruit you said was your favorite, but it does not mean they explicitly cared to remember. The line between both of them is the line of desire. Is someone important enough for you to want to remember things about them? Or do you want to improve your memory so nothing substantial about your dear ones ever skips your mind?

We all have ways devised for remembering. And I am sure some are quirky or silly, but as long as they work for you, no one has to know. For example, I currently walk around a track every day for 8 miles. I know that 2 ½ times around is a mile. So, I have to go around 20 times to reach my goal. Every time I complete a lap, I say to myself a word or phrase that I can associate with the lap # I just finished. I will say "one," as 1 is just the beginning. And with "two," I will make a peace sign with my fingers and look at it to also get a visual. Three might be "the Three Stooges." And for "four," I might say "Led Zeppelin Four" (their most popular album). I told you they might sound silly, but in this case, it works for me. Like most people, I had a step counter app on my phone, but had to remove it when it started talking at the most inopportune moments. Besides the mental exercise I came up with aides in improving my memory, like do math in your head instead of reaching for a calculator.

If I remember to make a daily list of the things I need to do, in theory, I won't forget to do everything on my list.

When it comes to directions, of course, we can always use "Waze" or "Google Maps". But if we go to the same place often enough, there's a less intrusive way than having your music constantly interrupted by the voice of your GPS. Also, Landmarks! Billboard signs, buildings, maybe restaurants, exits, and street signs, or even a crooked tree will begin to look very familiar after a few trips.

There are also other ways of improving your ability to remember things. Mnemonic devices are also a great way of improving long-term memory, so use acronyms, acrostics, and rhymes. You are more like to remember NASA than the National Aeronautics and Space Administration. Visual aids can also help, and keeping your brain sharp is another way of ensuring that you are at your best.

Memories help you relate to the world and the people around you. It turns them from strangers to loved ones, which is why it plays an important role in life. Not just so, but it also adds to your growth. 'Remember' that!

CHAPTER 30

READING PEOPLE—A PSYCHIC APPROACH

"Don't be foolish enough to judge a book by its cover."

I have known Dave for more than 30 yrs. He's a well-to-do, successful businessman who was out one day to buy a fancy new car. Dave likes nice things and has always had the ones as you see in the "Robb Report" or "Dupont Registery" magazines for as long as I have know him. One thing Dave is not is a fashion plate. His attire is always casual at most. So, when he walked into the local Ferrari dealership in a pullover shirt, shorts, and tennis sneakers, he almost seemed invisible, but only to the salespeople on the showroom floor as he looked over the new models. After 20 mins of waiting for a bit of assistance, which never came, he decided to exit. You see Dave has that, well, "I don't need you" money (as a kind way of saying it), some of which he used later that day at his friendly Porsche dealership. Since Dave also likes to rotate his cars, he may have wanted something Italian on a whim. I've seen a few of the Porsches he had before, so maybe another one was already in his sights as his plan B. At least one exotic car salesman had a good day at the office. So, you never know if the guy with the tennis sneakers is a tennis pro or just a wealthy person who is comfortable in sneakers.

Our eyes and our mind aid our life to a great extent. Our eyes process the things we see, and our mind processes them to the best of our abilities. It is through the example of Dave, and various other similar examples, that we understand that a majority of factors in life are multifaceted. "Things are not what they seem," as they say.

In such cases, having the gift of insight or reading people comes in handy. Seeing things and people and analyzing them to understand their true depth is an art, especially for human beings. We are all complex beings; we have a million things running in our minds in very short span. Our lives, too, are barely straightforward and hardly what it appears on the outside. This is why putting yourself in other people's shoes, or even sneakers comes not as a recommendation but as a necessity.

In the 1980 movie Caddyshack, think like a gopher scene, Bill Murray says, "I got to get into this dude's [the gopher] pelt and crawl around for a few days.

Even if we consider it professionally, careers in the field of psychology, or the field of understanding the mind, are booming. From mental health experts to psychologists, counselors and whatnot, the art of understanding human thoughts and emotions, of ourselves and others, is a precise skill. A society that operates together must understand the people and the minds in it. We also need to understand each other so we can know them better and mold ourselves accordingly.

If any of the salespeople at the Ferrari dealership had shown Dave a bit of interest, they just might have earned themselves perhaps a day's pay in a decent commission. Sadly, such was not the case. Dave was judged based on his 'comfortable' clothes that did not scream money, and everyone in the showroom took them at face value. If even one of them had not let their preconceived notions of what rich looks like cloud their judgment, their luck would have been much different that day. Similarly, the people around you are ready to offer you multiple chances. Maybe the person sitting next to you could be your soulmate or can be a great friend to you, but you'd never know it if you only see their jacket and judge that they do not match your standards. Things in life are not what they seem, and neither are people.

If you are one that might not have been given the gift of great insightfulness, maybe you possess a different stand-alone quality that you should be so proud of. Non-judgmental is being able to see everyone as equals without having to know their backstories. I have used the term "contempt before investigation," which is precisely what Dave's story is about—casting judgement without knowing all the facts. The bare facts, in this case, are that Dave has the means to buy *every* car on the showroom floor without any financing. But none of the salespeople at the Ferrari dealership would know that without showing him a little respect. The sad part is that no one there will ever know which model Porsche Dave purchased later that day, or more importantly, no one will learn from the costly mistake they all made in poor judgement.

CHAPTER 31

YOU ARE IN EVERY DEAL

"Only one word says selling like no other:
CONVINCING."

The stage of this book, from the very first chapter, has been set on holistically improving yourself so that you can "sell" yourself. The intention was to tell you how to market yourself and offer you various insights that aid you in doing so. But the entire premise of any sale starts with you. You are what you are selling, consciously or subconsciously. You present yourself to society every waking moment, engaging in it for survival. You are the object of the sale, and your contribution to society is the goods you have to offer to the world.

You enter the world to offer and sell your services and your goods. To do that, you must push yourself and your product through the door, so it can be seen. You use your services (the characteristics and qualities you possess) and pitch them to the world to find your "buyers," the ones who will receive your services. If communication between both parties (buyer & seller) is established, a pitch and connection are made through different communication mediums, like written, recorded, filmed, etc. But the ultimate point in your journey remains that you offer your product, and someone accepts it and allows you to present it to the audience. Your services turn different with different buyers (people you encounter in life). To some, you might be a teacher, and to a few, you have to play the role of a friend. You are to inhibit the qualities of an ideal employee to some, and for the "one," you are supposed to be the life partner. Your connection as a seller will be different with every buyer. Every situation will be different.

What you offer to someone will depend on the role they expect you to fill and what you hope to achieve in the end. For example, if you are going on a date, your focus will be on your looks, behavior, and overall personality. But if you sit down to take a math test, your concern will be your ability to solve the sums. Your mental math capabilities will hardly be of use on a date, and your good looks or humor will hardly be helpful in a math test. Hence, every situation is different, asking you to consider what qualities you have to put forward in a particular situation. Knowing so is also a vital part of the entire sales process. If you offer offering the wrong services to the wrong customers, it will be as good as useless.

Everyone offers their services by creating a wide range of competition. Every market is full of competition, from getting into a good university to getting a good job, to even finding a suitable person to spend your life with. It means what you offer must be different and better than the rest. Who will the universities pick if you get 80% in exams and your classmate scores 98% and has lots of extracurriculars? The answer is plain to see. Every market is full of competition, so we must always strive to improve ourselves to the best of our capabilities. Yet, know that there is only one way to improve yourself—honestly. If you try to "sell yourself" with false claims and promises, the results will be relatively short-lived. What you offer to the world and yourself has to be pure and true, based on the real qualities you possess. If there are things you do not possess yet and want to improve, this book is the key to helping you attain them. With each chapter, this book aims to help you make yourself a better product for yourself and the ones around you. You are your main product and your USP(unique selling point), so work on it to the best of your abilities and offer the world something only you can.

CHAPTER 32

I CAN'T BE EVERYONE'S FAVORITE

*"Proctor & Gamble knows that not everyone is going
to buy SCOPE, for many reasons (some pointless),
so they offer CREST and ORAL-B mouthwashes too."*

You can't be everyone's cup of tea, nor were you ever meant to be. There will be times in your life when you will be appreciated for all that you offer, but, at times, people won't see your merits no matter what you bring to the table. You could offer them more than they have had before, yet fingers will be pointed in your direction. Such situations can be extremely disheartening. No one would appreciate not being given their due, let alone not being treated with the praise they deserve. We run away from such situations or want to give up. Such thoughts crossing our minds are natural and not a sign of weakness. Yet how we deal with them genuinely showcases how strong or weak we are.

I can look back as a salesman and say 75% of my customers became my friends. That's a huge number. When I speak to a group, I strive for at least 60% of the floor. If I see the "bobbleheads" going up and down, I am happy and more adrenalized and motivated. Conversely, if I see just one "bobblehead" go side to side, that one can have a negative effect on how I'm doing. This is not politics, and certainly not today.

I've never been the only game in town in my chosen field. Sometimes the competition was much bigger. They may have had an advantage over me in every which way, but I may have something to offer that others don't want or need. Service, likeability, my integrity? The products, in most cases, are the same.

The next time you meet your friends, ask them to choose: vanilla, chocolate, or strawberry ice cream. Some might vote for chocolate, and some of the other two. In the end, everyone will have unique answers that might or might not match others. From this data, will you be able to decide which ice cream is the "best"? No! Because the answers are all subjective. Someone liking something based on their preference does not classify as an objective superiority over the other. As individuals, we all have different tastes and preferences. We form opinions easily and with little influence. Such cases do not present themselves as inherently in favor or opposition. There might be cases where the preferences favor you, and there might be cases where they offer you an edge.

Everyone would love to be loved. It is great to be admired and appreciated, adding brownie points to our likeability. But not being liked by all is also an important lesson. Some would argue that selling your product (yourself) means it must get out to the market at all costs; it must be bought and received. Yet no product is ever liked by all; there are products created simply for a targeted audience. In such cases, the focus shifts from selling the product to everyone to finding the niche audience. In life, too, a similar approach is to be followed. Find your audience and market yourself to them. Know who will appreciate the qualities you have to offer and who will need them. Do not waste your time, skills, and efforts on someone who cannot buy what you aim to sell. If you know someone is emotionally unavailable to be in a relationship, what good would it be for you to present yourself as a match? You will end up creating a disadvantage and degrade your value. Such a scenario is what we aim to avoid.

As a means of improving your likeability, the gift of being a good listener is a vital component in understanding the actual wants and needs of others. If such is not innate in your make-up, success in this can still be achieved with practice. Being mindful of what you hear is useful. In some cases, what might be perceived as criticism can be viewed and constructive.

So, how do we deal with situations that put us at a loss? How do we come out on top? The answer depends on what you consider the top in any scenario. There are no clean sweeps in life; remember that. Situations will sometimes be in your favor and sometimes not. The aim in these situations is not to try to change the mind of the people who do not want to buy what you offer but rather to focus on "repeated customers."

As a product, once you find your niche audience, the next challenge is sticking to it. This may seem boring or repetitive, but know that it is the secret weapon of making and breaking your product. Gone are those days when you had to engage in door-to-door selling techniques, a world where you would try to appease everyone. The world today is too self-centered for that. Open social networking sites, and you will see so many people embracing themselves as they are. Not just so, they use their uniqueness as their USP (unique selling point), distinguishing them from others around them and also creating their niche followers. The idea in the modern-day world is to create strong, steady, loyal, and life-long customers. That is what will aid you in the longer run.

Find people who appreciate you for what you are and what you offer. We are always an ongoing project, constantly working to better ourselves. Yet know that there is a difference between an audience that wants to watch you better yourself and an audience that wants you to change yourself. Find the ones who support your upward graph, and create a loyal customer base. If you are an employee and have the privilege to work for someone who allows you to grow professionally, take up that chance, such people are gems and rare. Even in your personal life, stay in touch with friends who appreciate your wins, small or big, rather than friends who want you to remain as a side character in their journey. The signs of knowing who is and is not your audience are always right in front of your eyes; you just need to look properly.

...btw, depending on which surveys you read, vanilla and chocolate flavor ice cream are interchangeable for the top spot.

CHAPTER 33

THE FUTURE TAKES TIME

*"The time we invest in worthwhile causes,
fill more than just our pockets."*

There's an old story about two wolves and a flock of sheep. Two wolves were viewing a herd of sheep from a hilltop. One said to the other, "if we storm the pack, we will probably each get a sheep." The other replied, "if we move in really slowly and quietly, we can have them all." This tale demonstrates a calculated approach to life and business on one level. A display of poise, patience, intuition, restraint, and calmness is prevalent.

The same story can be taken as a great lesson for how we live our lives.

"Slow and steady wins the race"—we have heard this at least a hundred times. It has been used repeatedly to teach us the importance of being consistent, investing time, and carrying out our actions meticulously. The tortoise, slow and steady, continuouslypersists through the hard times to ultimately achieve the winner's position. That is how humans are to work as well. In life, more often, things move at a slow pace.

Everything worth having comes with time and patience. If you want to speak a foreign language or learn a new skill, you know you cannot master it within a day or a few hours. You must dedicate yourself to the task at multiple sessions before witnessing the results. Not everything in life reaps positive results immediately. Success takes time.

Not to mention that the fast-paced world we live in has a lot more to offer to us than just monetary benefits and gain. Even though money is a major motivator in human life, it is not the only thing we achieve with time. Every experience ends up teaching us something. Good or bad, every moment lived is a lesson, and can be useful. It can teach you what you need to repeat to keep achieving success or inform you of what does not work for you. Not to mention that a lot of experiences that turn south end up teaching you more than the positive ones; they are the ones that push you to work harder and get out of your comfort zone.

One of the most essential factors that time has taught me when it comes to marketing myself and my product is networking as a skill. Time has taught me that patience yields great rewards. As I am marketing myself to the world, the buyers, aka the niche audience I invest in, are ultimately the seeds I am sowing that will reap me benefits in the future. At my workplace, neighborhood, friend circle, and society, I have realized that the relationships I form can take me exceptionally far.

Networking is a huge part of marketing. You know people who know people who know people who ultimately hear about you and might be interested in offering you an opportunity. Your good experiences with people will spread the word about you with time, and the same goes for any bad dealings. Examples of such can be seen on socialmedia. One bad experience, and nobody is shy of posting a review online for the entire world to see, potentially harming their image forever. To avoid that, it is essential to treat every single person with utmost respect and dignity. Take your time in building amiable relationships with everyone. It does not necessarily mean you must never speak against someone when they deserve it. But instead, your primary focus should be to always invest time in someone so they would be motivated to invest their loyalty in you. Both business and personal relationships work on this idea. Both require an investment of time, way more than any other factor. Money will come and go, but if you have taken the time to instill your loyalty and attention in someone, chances are that they will support you through the low times and add to your cheers in the high times.

Yet when the question comes to the investment of time, another factor that plays a 50% role is persistence. Every experience becomes knowledge. Good or bad, they can all be helpful. To remember and not to forget. Along with perseverance and resiliency, there's never a need to give up. We should be better today than the last time.

When I returned to work for my younger brother many years after I sold him the company, he reminded me of words I once told him, I should not give up on any prospective customer, no matter how small or big of a client they seem to be. Instead, I should invest my time in them and be persistent, which might result in them buying something from me tomorrow, if not today. The fact that he remembered that and used the lesson in business is evidenced by growing the company into the world's largest Gulfstream Jet parts business.

As a salesman, whether you have a product to sell or are marketing your self, you need to remember that every face you encounter is a potential customer. This is the same motto I followed when I first became a salesman in the early 80s. Back then, the newest marketing technique was to sell door-to-door, meaning I had no other option but to invest my time and persistence in every door. If I did not take my time and convince them enough, the door was shut in my face with no remorse. If I did well, I would be invited into the place of my new customer.

The ways might have changed, but the idea remains, and the world works the same. Are you willing to build your empire, one by one, with each customer and invest time and energy into them? If you do not, they will find someone else who will. We have already discussed the vast majority of competition in the world. Everyone has something to offer, and the only way you bring someone into your corner and keep them there is by showering them with genuine attention, patience, and dedication.

CHAPTER 34

COMPETITION IS EVERYWHERE

"Competition is small only when you have none."

In today's market, there is no limit to the options that present themselves in front of us. From face cream to an automobile, we have unlimited options to choose from in any given category. There is more supply than demand, meaning that the customer has turned into true royalty. They can choose your business, and if you fail to reach their standards, even 1%, there will be no hesitation in dropping you for someone better. Such an environment brings immense competition, but this competition is healthy. Not only does it keep everyone on their toes, but it also becomes the driving force of innovation. How many times have youseen something new hit the market, and suddenly you don't know which one it is because now there are 2 or 3 of nearly the same product out there already.

When a new competitor enters the arena, a frenzy is caused among all the players. They are no longer the only ones providing a service or product. So, the buyers who do not hold any particular connection to them will quickly run off to something better. This adds an unexpected change to the equation and creates a ripple effect where every part of the business must come together to fight the competition. At the initial stage, this might shake things up, but it is exactly this that ultimately keeps the business afloat. Know that no person or business can survive solely on stagnancy. With time and new waves of change, a conversion must also occur within. This transformation, aligned with the changes occurring outside us, acts as a catalyst for growth. In the end, competition benefits us as it promotes growth, innovation, and even the product you offer. It will help you thrive and adapt to the changing environment to keep up with the world around you. It will put you at pace with the competition and improve yourself. It will constantly teach you new skills and ways of the world, something you would never have done without competition.

It is competition and the change it drives that can alter how your business has been going. Not only can it aid you in improving a product that already exists, but it also can cause you to create something entirely new. Multiple examples of this are noted in the books of history. Case in point—Viagra, that today stands to be the number one erectile dysfunction medicine, was initially invented by Pfizer as a heart medicine. And this invention then opened the doors for Eli Lilly's Cialis and Bayer's Levitra. Likewise, it was competition and change that prompted John D. Rockefeller to create gasoline as his Standard Oils lamp oil business dried up with the introduction of electricity… just in time for Henry Ford's Model T. And even NASA, in their need to create the best, has laid claims to around 2000 spinoff products, some of them being freeze-dried food, fireman suits, and memory foam.

Competition is the way to innovation. Change and challenge must go hand in hand to drive excellence. You must always take competition as a nudge to do better. Never be discouraged and disheartened in the face of challenge. Use it to excel, and watch yourself create wonders.

Here it might be safe to say, "behind every good or bad product is a good or bad person." Humanity is at the center of everything we create, so humanity is, therefore, what drives us. From getting into a good university grabbing a good job to even finding a good enough person to spend your life with, every market is full of competition, even the "people" market.

CHAPTER 35

CLOSE THE DEAL, NOT THE DOOR

*"Always put forth your best pitch. You may be the
only game in town until you find out you're not!"*

In the sales world, there will always be people who are almost-salespeople meaning that they 'almost' make the sale but never actually make it. The difference between these two is the true mark that turns you from an almost-salesperson to a successful salesperson. If you dance with the customer for too long, never trying to finalize the deal, they will find someone else who can provide them with the sameservice for much less hassle. It then comes down to; you must ask for the order and know how and when to ask, or you may never get it. It's having or getting a feel for it. I learned this from experience. Remember, the customer needs the product, which must always come before you need for sale. If you push too hard, their needs will be filled by the competition. Such is the reality of making a sale. And then, just providing a product is not the only job of a salesperson; they need to ensure that the product provided is as cost-effective and time-saving as possible, and of course, what they bargained for and expected.

As a young salesman just starting work in this field, I had to learn this lesson the hard way. The dance of actually making a sale is a very calculated one. You must know what you sell and how to do it to benefit you and your customer. Remember, the customer needs the product, so they will be willing to dance with you. But beware! If you do not do it right, they will find a different partner, a seller who will give them more pros than you offer. When I began my career as a salesman, my focus was set on making long-term friendships and relationships. I wanted every customer to be at ease and get to know me and I them, so I invested a lot of time in building relationships. Playing golf, ballgames, dinner, and lunches, etc., were all a part of my plan. I would make some good friends at the end of the day but it didn't always translate into a business partner. They would find someone offering them a better deal, whereas I was busy offering them a cordial relationship.

This, in no way, showcases that you should not aim to build relationships in life and business. On the contrary, it is a great tactic or strategy to develop good relationships and long-term friendships. Yet, often I would end up shy with deals closed; I had to remind myself that your business should be 50-50. You have to think of the customer's gain, but you must think of your own. Your business is not a charity case, and the same applies to your life. Everything in life, just like a sales pitch, should be 50-50 from both parties involved. If you are giving something, you should get something in return. Being friendly in life is important, but ensure you do not end up getting too far removed from your goal. Ultimately, your aim is to make a sale, not just interaction.

Closing the door on the deal as opposed to closing a deal may or may not be your making. Everything you do affects your sales, and every decision can alter how the deal goes. The best way to close the deal is to be truthful and be yourself.Offer your best and ensure it does not put someone else in a con.

CHAPTER 36

THE ART OF CONTENTMENT

*"Don't let the accolades or the material things
change you. They all can go away someday,
but who you are inside remains."*

Life is all about struggling and overcoming the challenges that we face. We work hard, jump over the hurdles that stand in our way, and ultimately aim to provide our life something better than it has had before. Being able to buy the things we have always had our eye on is usually everyone's measure of success. Affording the house you always wanted, the phone you dreamed of, and the car you loved are all our measures of having 'made it'.

Yet the privilege and achievements we earn in life also seem to be very subjective. Someone might take their beauty as an achievement and do the same for their fame. It is human nature to consider these things as positive, as it cannot be denied that such things do bring us extra opportunities. If you are attractive, chances are that you will draw more attention to yourself than someone who is not on the same level. Your chances of having your pick amongst dating partners would also be higher, but that does not ensure you are the best candidate in the long run.

If you aren't emotionally **fit** and mentally intelligent, your good looks can only take you so far. A similar saga can be seen for the famous ones in this world. If we see someone famous, our curiosity will get the best of us, and we will want to know more about them than any other average human. All such instances are parts of human nature, which always aims to achieve more. We want to be prettier, richer, smarter, famous, etc.

"Movin' on up"—The Jeffersons—1975-1985

We run after money to replace the things we already have with nicer things. If we have Converse All-Stars, then we want Air Jordans. We want to replace our Toyota with Mercedes, Maybelline with Chanel. Every achievement we grab, unlocks a new desire, causing us to dream of something better. The problem arises when we realize that this replacement process never ends. There will always be a better thing to want, a shinier thing to need, and a costlier object to attain. In this rat race, before we realize it, we end up shedding away our modesty and letting greed overpower us. When you feel yourself never being satisfied with what you have, know that it is time to stop.

Do you know that Sam Walton, of Walmart fame, drove a Ford F-150 pickup? Or that J. Paul Getty, even after earning so much in life, used to bring his lunch in a brown paper bag? Letting yourself sway with the materialistic pleasures in life is extremely easy, but exactly as difficult is grounding yourself to not lose humility. Life can offer you everything you need but not everything you want. Hence, your sights should not be to be the richest or prettiest or most famous, but rather to be comfortable and proud of how far you have come. If you remember your roots, the journey upward will always be easier. You will be moving with an aim to do your best, not to achieve the best over others.

If we can be content with what is within our reach, then we are right where we should be. We need to unhesitatingly appreciate all that we possess, and know that being grateful for how far we have come is a non-negotiate step. Let the power of genuine gratitude push you, and you will realize that it gives you calmness and drive. Be humble and see how far you will go.

CHAPTER 37

POLITICS AND RELIGION— WHAT DOES IT MATTER ANYWAY

"Religion is a choice no one has to make.
Politics is the choice most quietly make."

Whenever the topic comes to politics or religion, the entire room is shushed extremely quickly. Why is it that we are so vary of ever calmly discussing both of these topics? And if any discussion is ever had on both of them, the result is either of the three—1) Both parties hold the same viewpoint, but it still does nothing to bring them closer as humans. 2) Both parties are strongly at odds with each other, resulting in hatred that may lead to violence. Or 3) Both of them are indifferent. No matter the outcome, the chances of the conversation going astray and leading to negative results are always higher than it brings people closer. Hatred always sparks a fire better than love does. Multiple acts of communal violence in the history books are a testament to such a fact.

Both of these factors—politics and religion, -started out in the name of improving humanity, yet not all of us are sure it can be claimed in today's time. With either case, what should always matter in the long run is how people are treated, whether it is the political beliefs of one person or the religion they practice. No religion promotes supremacy, but all talk of living in communal harmony. So, despite what religion you practice or even if you are an atheist, the goal is to always be tolerant of other's religious freedoms and mode of expression.

I saw an example of it a few years ago, which taught me that decent stood way above par than religious or political.

I was out one day with a friend for dinner at a fancy restaurant where we were joined by two priests who knew my friend. The conversation soon started, and soon I was talking about how someone owed me a large amount of money, and I was having trouble collecting it. The young stocky priest, sitting right next to me, went quiet. After a few seconds, he turned to me and said, "All I need is a name and the town, and I'll assist you in getting your money." A chill went down my spine, understanding what he meant, but since I wasn't onboard with his thinking, I laughed it off. He took the hint and changed subjects, but the entire experience taught me that there is no use of putting labels of religions, believes, or politics on self if we do not even follow the basic concepts of humanity that they preach.

Throughout my existence, I have always felt "People will kill for love and money". I believe this could have also been said, but I can't find any evidence of such a quote. You see, I thought this might have applied during the times when Kings and Queens, Rulers, and Emperors ruled the lands. What I've witnessed today, and like never before,

The influence of greed and power dement the truth in one's character who stands without conscience.

CHAPTER 38

SPIRITUALITY FROM OZ

"I believe everyone has a touch of spirituality to help them find themselves and their place in this world. Such consciousness is like the bubble in a level."

Whenever I am faced with whether or not I am religious, the answer that comes to me is always "no, but I am spiritual." People, then, look weirdly at me because they are the same thing in their books. Yet a difference exists between the two, which seems monumental simultaneously. Yes, it cannot be ignored that religion and spirituality are connected, but there still is a vast difference between them. Religion is a choice, but spirituality is not; it resides within all of us if we can recognize it. In both cases, there is a God or an identity that I prefer to call the "Creator." In religion, people choose to worship the beliefs of a structured group. There are guidebooks, idols, and places to worship. Spirituality, on the other hand, is about awareness. It is an awareness of the ongoing connection with our creator and the creator of all things around us and beyond. With spirituality, you realize that you are created to exist as a small component of everything around you.

You are on an assignment to play a preplanned role in this systematic world and share in harmony what has been in place before you.

Even the word "awareness" is undoubtedly one of my favorites. Awareness is an essential and vital part of spirituality; one cannot exist without the other. In combination, both are about seeking, searching, and wondering, and all of them are different ways that ultimately lead you to find who you are inside. As a part of our spirituality, awareness is a state of mind, a feeling, or even an aura. It takes us on a journey that leads us to wonder what everything around us is there for? It wills us to discover the balanced and systematically-designed surroundings that exist around us, something we might not have noticed before. It leads us to understand who we are and why we act and behave the way we do. Awareness and spirituality make us realize that we have a role in this world. We are to live the way the creator wanted us to live—to the best of our abilities.

The journey of spirituality leads you to know, understand, and worship yourself so you can mold yourself into your best version. There are no set books or rules you are to follow. No particular practices exist for you to engage in, and no deities that you must donate money to. Spirituality, instead, puts you as the ruling factor. You are to become your judge and make yourself a good person. You should know what is right and wrong for you, and the false words of the world outside must not sway you. All these practices of reaching awareness are preached to you through spirituality, which is why I prefer it over a particular religion with its dos and don'ts. This book is intended to push you towards the road of spirituality, not in an obsessed way, but with a gentle nudge so you end up changing yourself as you require.

One of my favorite movies in the world is The Wizard of Oz. The movie is based on the children's novel, "The *Wonderful* Wizard of OZ," written by L. Frank Baum in 1900. Two years following the fairytale book's release, a play was cast on Broadway, "The Wizard of Oz," and the ever-popular movie with the commonly adopted name in 1939. I have seen the movie multiple times, and every time I see it, I admire the message it conveys. The story tells us that we all have a heart, brain, and a level of courage that stands beyond the limitations of our fears. Yet many of us cannot realize this and reach our full potential. We do not see the path that waits for us to walk on it so we can become better. This path only exists if we allow it to exist; it will only be there if we do not convince ourselves that we are too tired to find it. Our dreams can always remain in our sights, so we must work towards finally achieving them. We must dodge the bad apples life throws at us. Persevere and do what it takes. Our spirituality, if we stay true to it, will help us guide ourselves through all challenges. All we have to do is believe in it.

HUMOR

CHAPTER 39

SMILE, LAUGHTER IS FUNNY BUSINESS

*"When someone is funny, people have a way of
letting you know, especially if you're not."*

The art of having a sense of humor has evolved with time. From the age of royalty having a jester in their court to the Netflix stand-up specials we see today, the 'funny' world has drastically changed. What has remained, however, is the timelessness of the concept of humor. Even if we talk of the comedians of modern time, we have seen many of them go from comedy clubs to the small or big screen. Eddie Murphy, Steve Martin, Jim Carrey, Michael Keaton, Billy Crystal, Emma Thompson, and many more are now known by the entire country and worldwide. And we love them and other comedians so much because comedy has the power of reaching our hearts in the most wholesome way. There is no person in the world who doesn't love to laugh and be carefree, and comedy lets us reach that stage. It allows us to enjoy life and reminds us that it is a core value that should be instilled in us all.

Humor was so popular and important in the film industry. Live audiences were used to get television audiences to laugh. And in 1953, Charles Douglass invented the "Laff Box" so that recorded laughs could be added to sitcoms and cartoons to get viewers to bite on funny filmed productions. Someday watch the "Flintstones," "Mr. Ed" (the talking horse), or the "Munsters" if you want a good smile at this invention in action.

But be wary if someone says you're funny. It can also have a very negative connotation. In the movie "Goodfellas," Joe Pesci says to Ray Liotta, "How am I funny." Great Scene. That was funny in a negative way. Or George Thorogood in the song "One Bourbon, One Scotch, One Beer." He said, "I don't know, man; ah, she's kinda funny, you know." I said, "I know, everybody's funny. Now you're funny, too."

Yet humor is not just restricted to telling jokes. Studies have shown that laughter is also way more than just an act. There are health benefits that come with good laughter. Think of what happens when you laugh. Your muscles contract, and you take in more oxygen. Your heart rate increases, and the endorphins in your brain begin to flow. You become less stressed; thus, anxiety is suppressed. The cause for your laughter stimulates your brain. In a group you bond with others who are laughing. The only hazard of a good laugh might be falling off your chair!

If laughter is the best medicine, as most will agree, its subtler form, a smile, also holds just as much power. A smile has a sneaky power, one many might not be aware of. A smile can have the power to improve someone's day and make it better. If you pass a smile to a stranger on the road, they will smile back. Even if they had been walking with a frown, they might be friendly to you, which will uplift their mood. That is the power of a smile. And it doesn't have to be a single occurrence. So, why not let that be your way, your signature first expression all the time? This was so evident with a girl I knew well. She smiled every time our eyes met. I can honestly say that's why I dated her. However, I don't understand why she dated me back. I guess I was funnier than my smile.

Getting someone to smile is the result of the by-product of a positive connection. You don't always need to make someone have a belly laugh for you to form a connection. A smile can do that for you. Moreover, a smile can create a connection, whether one on one or even with an entire audience. If you are nervous about giving a presentation in a room full of people, you will feel at ease if you see someone smiling at you. If nobody does that and you face a room full of frowning people, your nervousness will spike up. If you see a sign of a smile, you instantly know it is a display of approval. Watch them give a nod and see the situation is in your favor. Even if you are in a situation that has nothing to offer you, a smile can defuse the problem if it is tense. It could make the environment lighter if there is awkwardness in the air or offer you solace if you are looking for relief. A small muscle movement has so much to offer to this world and also to you. Just as you would love to be on its receiving end, engage in it to be the giver.

Whether you are the one in a position of power or the one at others' mercy, a smile will always be there as a great icebreaker. A can relax a room and make you come across as friendly and likable. For example, on your first day of work, if you approach your new coworkers with a serious look, nobody would warm up to you easily. Instead, they would be wary of the new guy who seems too serious. But if you approach the same event with a smile, your coworkers will go away with a good first impression, affecting how they work with you in the future.

Passing a smile costs you nothing, yet it can give you everything if you let it. So, realize its true power and engage it. Afterall, why so serious?

CHAPTER 40

SOME JUST TRY TOO HARD

"You don't have to be funny if that is not you."

This book has abundant discussion on humor and all the power it holds. The power of humor can get us through many doors in life. Whether it is a club, a friend group, an attractive person, or even a job, everyone appreciates a good sense of humor. The key word is 'good.' People only laugh with you if you are funny. If not, they won't be afraid of laughing at you. A good sense of humor has to come from within.

Sadly, it cannot be mimicked or faked. It is an asset only if it is genuine. It will not be appreciated if you try too hard and force people to laugh at your jokes. The world around you is always quick to judge, which is why how we navigate it has to be innovative.

Though people do not usually appreciate it, it is understandable that others try to mimic this quality as a natural tendency. If the world admires the ones who are funny, the ones who are not would also be willing to be so. But when you are placed in such a situation, know that being who you are is better than pretending to be something you are not. Trying to emulate someone else or copying characteristics, especially something as delicate as humor, will never do true justice to your character. Nor will it raise your bar as everyone around you will be able to witness that the act put on is not genuine.

Human beings are smart creatures and can easily detect when someone isn't genuine. They have a great tendency to catch such hints. This is why being who you are is the best way to go in any situation. One such example is reality shows. I remember being in a sports bar where one of the many TVs showcased "Jersey Shore". I am not a fan of the reality show, but being from New Jersey and having spent a lot of time down the shore, it was hard not to pay attention. As I watched, even if only for a few minutes, I could conclude that almost all the people in the show were running to act in a way they certainly were not. Everyone in the cast, no matter who, looked and talked like each other. Everyone wanted to be cool on screen, and the desperation was quite evident, turning me away as a viewer.

When you try too hard, it's usually obvious. As I said, wanting to be liked is a human condition, and mimicking qualities the audience genuinely tends to love is a common occurrence. But we must understand that in a world of plastic, genuineness is appreciated more than any other quality. Just like how a conversation or friendship cannot be forced, humor has to come naturally. It should not be forced for the sake of it, or it will simply appear too unnatural. Be who you are and watch people appreciate you for just that.

CHAPTER 41

INSECURITIES ON DISPLAY

*"When you need all the attention,
you may get it. But how you get it lets
everyone know what it's doing to you."*

I remember every day at the office started with me witnessing an exhibit put on by a coworker. Every morning, for our entertainment pleasure, she walks into the room a little later than everyone else. I am certain the act is intentional on her part, as it allows her to make a grand entrance. As heads turn her way, she is satisfied and, with her pageant walk, she moves to take a seat. There, she snaps a few selfies, which undoubtedly end up on social media even before the meeting. As if this routine isn't predictable enough, she gets up from the meeting at least two-three times in between.

Once is usually to use the bathroom, probably to check her hair and make-up; others are often to throw something away, or to get coffee. The kitchen area is across the room, but she is probably glad it is. I think she brings something to throw out every morning, so she has a prop with her. The routine may vary in detail, but the essence of it remains the same every single day. She relies on false confidence to draw all the attention her way. It is the emotional fuel that fills the emptiness she so desperately has.

"Do you know who some people impress most? Only themselves. Sometimes they are their only audience, it seems."

She is an attractive young woman who knows she is attractive, yet her actions do not seem to agree. Her constant displays of turning the topic to herself make the rest of the world aware that she is treading in a quicksand of low self-esteem. Her actions are her effort to climb out. She wants validation from others to be the rope that pulls her out, but confidence does not work that way. The attention that she relies on ends up transforming itself into false confidence. If others look at her and pay attention, she thinks she is worth something. If not, she sees herself as worthless. Such dependency on others must be taking an emotional toll on her confidence, which is blatantly visible in her actions.

The problem stems from the fact that she is one of many to do so. A lot of the younger generation today struggles with self-confidence and, ultimately, self-worth issues. Like her, many people in this world end up putting airs about themselves and putting on a show for others, not to realize that their insecurities still seep through their actions. Self-confidence shines from within, and if you do not have it, the desperation of trying hard is easily visible. Not just so, but trying too hard does not ensure that the job is done. She must have assumed that making a grand entry or taking breaks within minutes must cause everyone else to view and bask in her importance. Yet it actually creates a nuisance within the meeting where everyone wishes for her to stop.

Instead, to gain attention, she should focus on her work and present brilliant ideas that blow us away. A confident person would not resort to such tactics to make themselves seen. Their ideas and work speak for themselves, being the envy and the inspiration for others. So, if you want to shine, start building yourself from the core, not just the outer layer.

A TIME AND A PLACE

"Timing is everything, with everything."

"There is a time and place for everything"—how many times have we heard the phrase? Like anything, "there's a time and place" for everything. This is an equation having three variables. A "TIME"— when it's appropriate. A "PLACE"—being the location or setting. And the "EVERYTHING", which is the action part. Being mindful, or just simply aware through experience, is our guide on how to act.

This weightage of importance is also why getting all three right is very tricky. We often end up performing the right task at the wrong place or even saying something at the wrong time. There are no set rules for all three, yet the experience teaches us what is right and what is wrong. "Don't laugh at a funeral," "Don't tell someone they are closer to death on their birthday," "Don't be rude to someone to their face"—the list goes on forever. This list, too, has been carved from human experiences.

Experience is all we need. It is the constant factor for all outcomes in this equation. The "everything" is whether to clap or not, and experience lets us know if it's okay to clap or to stand down. When you're at the dentist, and there's music playing, it's always "elevator music", not heavy metal. So, every situation and every setting has to have the "right" feel or tone. But we also know smiling or crying at a funeral is okay.

And if it's your own, you'll never know how funny you were when you couldn't hear them having fun.

It's not always easy or obvious to understand how we should act and behave in every circumstance. There is specific decorum for every setting. So how are we to know what's correct right here or now? We mainly draw from our experience or what others teach us.

Knowing what to do and when to do it is the skill that can turn any ordinary human into a successful one. The right timing can shape your life if you let it. Our intuition and experience often tells us what to do and when not to do it. With experience, you will probably not play death metal in a hospital or throw a tantrum when someone is walking down the aisle. It teaches you that initiating tasks at work has the power to make you seen by the boss, or helping others will ensure a clear conscience. The timing makes or breaks everything if you know how to follow through with its signals.

CHAPTER 43

I'M NO ONES JOKE

"No one can make you feel inferior
without your consent."

If knowing when to make a joke is important, then it is just as important as knowing when to take one. This necessarily does not mean that every joke cracked at your expense will make you laugh. The differentiation, however, is in how you take it. Life is not fair, and neither is everyone else. Unfortunately, there are a lot of people in life who will mistreat you to compensate for their own inadequacies. In multiple instances, these compensations may be disguised as jokes. If you take offense, they will tell you are being too serious and should "lighten up a little."

Knowing when I am the object of a joke or when it says something more profound is what experience will teach you. If you book tickets to see a comedian that operates on including the audience in their show, then you have to be prepared that you might be a harmless target for the night. But if the same jokes, or even worse ones, are cracked on you in an office or any such setting, you will not want to dismiss them as simple humor. Chances are that the latter has already happened to you at least once. People are insecure beings, which is why they pick on others to make themselves feel at ease. You might have had a classmate, a friend, or a coworker who uses you as their punching bag.

A similar situation happened to me when an acquaintance who loved to put me down in front of our peers. He would always say digs at me, and when I tried to interject to tell him to cut the crap, he would always tell me that he didn't mean anything by it. The funniest part was that when he and I were alone, he would try to act friendly with me, trying to get in my good books. But I knew better. However, as this continued, a friend told me in confidence that he was jealous of me. I was the subject of admiration of our peers, not him, which made him insecure, and he tried to take that insecurity out on me. I sympathized with him but knew I had to put him in his place to end this charade.

Us humans are inherently jealous and insecure beings. It takes a lot of effort to train our minds not to let such ideals get the best of us. There will always be someone better than us, but the way to deal with this jealousy can never be petty. If you are in such a situation where you need to use someone else as your punching bag, know that it will, in the end, not do anything for your self-esteem. You will only put yourself in a bad light, worsening your self-esteem.

If you are in a position where someone tries to use you as the subject of their harmful jokes, know that you are above them. Someone sees you as a better opponent, which is why they try to bring you down to their level. Do not allow them to do so. As Eleanor Roosevelt said, "No one can make you feel inferior without your consent." Know that you can stand up for yourself if the situation gets worse. But above all, nobody except yourself, can make you feel bad about yourself. No one has the power to control your feelings.

HAPPINESS

CHAPTER 44

WE ARE ALL SOCIAL BEINGS

"I can do this thing, with or without you.
But it would be better with you."

We are all individualistic, keeping our goals and aspirations in the main line of vision. Usually, this outlook deludes us into believing that we can exist simply as individuals and not as part of our society. Such thinking needs to be squashed at its initial stage. When you look closely, it becomes clear that all of us, while existing in our circle, also are a vital part of the circle that ends up creating our society. One person cannot move a boulder, but a lot together can. Life works in the same way. You might assume that you are pushing with more vigor and energy, and your push may account for more. Yet eventually, it is everyone's combined effort that counts.

Think of yourself as an individual in a socially cooperative existence. But how do you uphold your "end" as just one small "moving" part in God's-devised system? Working with others to improve our surroundings so that we thrive and grow this planet.

Focusing on the phenomenon from an individualistic point of view rather than a worldviewmakes it clear that we need people around us to exist. In my book, I Didn't Ask to be Me; I outlined the concept by highlighting how people need people. I mentioned the detriments of self-isolation and how it can eventually take a toll on an individual for the worse. There, too, exists various case studies in the world to showcase this not to mention that an obvious example can be the movie, Tarzan. It is too simple, yet it gets the point across.

The essence of it all is that people need people. Staying too far away from humans for too long can become caustic—an example of why solitary confinement in prison is the most tortuous penalty for any inmate. Being away from society and the "human element" eventually affects the mind and the body, creating stagnancy in both. We need to communicate, share, and exchange our feelings with others. Michael Platt, a Ph.D scholar from the University of Pennsylvania Perelman School of Medicine, said that "human beings are wired to connect— and we have the most complex and interesting social behavior out of all animals."

Even if some of us were hesitant to believe the phenomenon before, the lockdown initiated by the COVID-19 pandemic ended up proving it to us. When we were locked in our homes, we realized how important it was to be out in the world and interact with society. Whether it was insignificant in the long run or something consequential from the beginning, the whole era of the pandemic instated the fact in us. Even if I were to go by my example, being out and around people has always given me energy. I no longer have a 9-5 job that keeps me connected to people every day. Though it has perks, mandatory interaction with others has taken a considerable blow. Because of this, I now reach out to people whenever I can, no matter how small of an interaction.

Even back home in New Jersey, there are a few restaurants where I am a "regular." I have eaten at them for half my life and have also made friends and acquaintances there. I know most of the regulars, the waiters, and the bartenders. And they know me, passing me a smile every time I am there. It's "Cheers" to me. They know what I like to order and ask me about my life. I, too, ask them about theirs, and this small talk, sometimes leading to longer and deeper conversations, have a way of reconnecting me to the world around me. It can reenergize me and make me see myself as a part of the bigger circle of society.

I remember bringing a girl to my favorite restaurant, Il Villaggio's, in Carlstadt, NJ one night. The bar where I usually sit is off to the side in the big dining room. I still wanted to eat at the bar, but I spotted someone I knew at a table as soon as we broke into the dining room from the marble foyer. I said, "I have to say "hi" to someone, okay." She followed me over, so I could introduce her to the table. I spotted another, and then another, and proceeded to go from table to table until none were left. She said, "do you own this place?" I laughed while saying, "no." We ate there many times since that night, and she became my girlfriend shortly after. I think it was the sauce!

Humans are meant to be acquaintances, friends, partners, family, and more. We are meant to be around each other, existing in the same circle, even when we want to be left alone. We thrive when we are with each other. We are, after all, social beings.

RELATIONSHIPS: LASTING LOVE, OR VERY CLOSE FRIENDS

"There is a place we can go, but how far we'll figure out when the time is revealed."

If human beings cannot exist in isolation, it is necessary to pay attention to their relationships. Yet, when it comes down to it, the question of sexual instincts is the biggest one to be answered. The basic instincts of humans are always sexual. It drives our mind to constantly be looking for the "one." The possibility of procreating and finding companionship in that pleasure is our greatest quest.

In every possible beginning of a relationship, the idea of sex always drives us forward, which is why boundaries and clarity on the idea should be established before entering a relationship. For example, when you meet someone new, are you initiating the relationship to end up as friends or companions? Before entering the relationship arena, you need to understand and acknowledge the distinction between the two. There are certain questions you are to ask yourself: Are you aiming for a long-term relationship? Or is the relationship meant to be on short-term implications? Which peak do you eventually hope to reach in the relationship, and on what terms?

These might seem like dreadful questions, pushing your mind to get serious before you hope to. It is, however, the answer to all of them that is needed to know which direction you are to guide the relationship in, especially when it comes to sexual understanding. You can date someone, be just friends with them, see them as a younger sibling, or might not be sexually attracted to them at all. Such feelings must be distinguished at the beginning to avoid any difficulties that might erupt later. As well as they are to help your mind guide itself in controlling or unleashing your sexual tendencies. When your mind is aware that you are looking at someone only as a friend, that they are unavailable for a sexual relationship, it will train itself to be in control. On the other hand, if you know someone single and you are interested in them, you would want to shoot your shot.

Our mind is so fogged up by our sexual desires that we have found a way around the commitment that comes with it. In the new age, we have created 'friends with benefits. As the name suggests, it allows all the pleasure of a physical, sexual relationship without the commitments of a romantic one. Various other ways around it, through it, curving it, and circling it, have been created by humanity. This, once again, proves that we inherently are a sex-driven race who must have our need fulfilled at any cost.

Because one of our human instincts is sexual, as relatable as anything else in this book, finding that "one" in your life, possibly to procreate with or for necessary companionship as in pleasure, may be our greatest quest. I heard that only humans have sex for pleasure (except for dolphins and the Bonobos monkey that also do). Do dogs think will impregnate someone's leg, a chair, or a stuffed toy?

In our run behind it, we, however, end up neglecting many factors that should be in our focus. We allow sex to ruin good relationships and friendships. We allow its pleasure to push us to cheat in our relationships or ruin good ones. It is powerful but just as lethal, so knowing what you want out of a relationship becomes an inevitably important one. The unveiling of your intentions with a new relationship is inevitable and quite necessary. The timing here is critical if there is to be a courtship on any level. You may already have a short script in your head, but it must be honest. It's people's feelings we're dealing with here. Yet most of all, both your flight plans need to match. If you don't share the same mutual intent, each destination will be different. This might be best accomplished as soon as possible. Remember, people have feelings!

CHAPTER 46

THIS IS HOME

"Home is where you are missed most
and where you miss the most."

What is a home? Is it a house or a street address for you? Maybe it's as big as your country of birth. Well, if you are asked, most will eventually say that home is not merely a place but rather a feeling. Home is where we feel like our most honest selves are allowed to be who we are. We are at one with our surroundings, knowing it in and out and basking in its comfort. For some, this home is their parents or their family. For others, it can be their friends or the city they grew up in. Everyone has a different definition of home, but the essence of all remaining the same brings you peace.

When living in Atlanta, I would make it a point to go back home to New Jersey a few times a year. This was where I grew up and spent most of my life. So, whenever I was in town, I would visit family, friends, and even acquaintances I knew growing up and hanging out there.

I even spent a little time in the out-of-season, staying at a friend's house beach house that was closed for the winter because I wanted a peaceful place where I could write. It was very cold at the shore, so I could only see the ocean through panes of glass. But, like Hemingway at the Keys, I felt like a pent-up author in a bungalow by the beach, in a desolate ghost town by the dunes created by the winds of a wintery ocean. By the way, it wasn't a bungalow I stayed at. It was a great new house in one of the most affluent towns on the Jersey shore, where I slept on the most comfortable mattress of my life. But I did paint a writer's picture of my stay "by the seaside".

The first place that came to mind when the opportunity presented itself was to go back to New Jersey. The people back home treated me like I was special. They all genuinely seemed happy to see me, and even when I was visiting after long, they made me fit right in as I had never left. Many of them told me that I looked good, whichinitially seemed weird as I had recently gained a little weight. But soon I realized what they meant because, yes, I probably looked fine. Moreover, I had looked happy. I was back home, and that fact alone filled me with so much contentment.

As I mentioned, home is a feeling. It gives you comfort and contentment, and it is up to you to find your home. Yet, in many situations, it is impossible for us to return to our hometowns or wherever we might have felt at home. Being an adult comes with its own set of responsibilities, and sometimes what we want to do and what we are to do clash. In such cases, the focus should be on driving through. Then, when the time gets tough, we are to sear through it to ultimately find what we are looking for. Home, too, is such a similar concept. If we keep searching for it in someone else or someplace where we cannot be, we will remain disappointed and depressed. But if we recognize that we have the power to be our own homes and create comfort for ourselves, we can change the peace we derive from the world around us.

Your mind has to play an important part in creating this home around you. I don't have kids, but I have plants and wild birds & squirrels I tend to every day. I water or feed them and watch them grow. My mind recognizes the part I play in keeping them alive and healthy. Not just so, but all such small yet significant acts are important in making ourselves comfortable in our skin giving us peace. We must make ourselves our home, no matter where we are in the world. Love yourself and treat yourself. Engage in self-care. I like to write, but I also want to take a break when there's a good movie on. It's good to turn off all the technology that surrounds us once in a while and focus on enjoying the moment.

We get so wound up with life in our brains and bodies, so it's essential to unwind from it all once in a while. Being productive every minute can lead to being unproductive when we don't rest and recharge.

No matter where you are, engage in self-care and create your peace. Here are a few tips you can follow:

- Paint your life green: You are a part of nature, and it is very important for you to realize it. Tend to it as you tend to your self. Water it and take care of it. Watch it bloom and realize that none of it would be possible without your help.

- It's all in the balance: Life will never be fun if it is all about work, work, work. No matter how much you like your work, you must detach yourself from it and create a balance. You work to live; you don't live to work.

- Bye-bye gadgets: Like I just mentioned, it is good to detach yourself from the devices in your hand. We use these devices so much that it feels like they are glued to our fingers, but every once in a while, remind yourself that that is not the case. Switch off your phone or put it on silent. Place it in a different room and enjoy your conversation with your loved ones. The world won't end if you don't check your notifications every two minutes.

- Find things that make you happy: If you like something, stick to it. It does not necessarily need to be a profitable act, and you do not even need to be great at it. If you like painting, paint. You can be a terrible painter, but as long as it relaxes you, that is all that matters. Find things you love and do it just for the heck of it.

THE ALL-ROUNDED WINNER

*"In a world filled with all kinds of winner types,
the clearest I see are the well-rounded ones. Wise and
smart enough to know when to make you laugh."*

"Who will you choose?"—No matter the position, this question will inevitably stand in front of us. Whether we are interviewing for a job position, a friend, or a potential mate, our mental checklist shines at the forefront. It tells us what we appreciate in a person and what we do not. Humans love to judge the ones around us, which is why we are always critical of everyone we meet. We critique how someone laughs, walks, looks, behaves, and everything on the panel. Even their IQ and sense of humor is found on most lists. Being a very important factor, might I add.

So who DO we choose? The choice might be situational and for specific circumstances, but the model for whatever case has many commonalities. Over the years, I have observed and concluded there is a mental checklist with any candidate considered. A job, a mate, a position chosen that fits the bill. Even in a beauty pageant, there's more than meets the eye in the winner.

Did you ever hear this one… "but she has a good personality." That could only be construed as a disparaging remark. And for most, it's shallow of anyone who uses that response with any new encounter. It wreaks insecurity on their part. But others are able to see that "good personality" in someone without having their looks weigh so heavily in your thoughts of them.

When asked whom my friend wants his daughters to marry someday, he replied that somebody who is well-rounded, smart, and with a good head on their shoulders. Someone who is not too stuffy. Someone with a sense of humor. Physical appearance was never mentioned, which supports a hierarchy of importance. But like anything in life, there are exceptions. Intelligence might not be as important as brawn when looking for a mover. And similarly, muscles and stamina have less importance when looking for a programmer.

When you are looking for someone to join your company, you might want someone competent. If you are to look for a partner, you look for someone kind or even attractive. No matter what kind of a checklist it is, it cannot be ignored that a trait none of us can ignore is being well-rounded. We can appreciate someone who is intelligent, funny, but we will always appreciate someone smart and funny rather than alone. Being all-rounded allows us to walk through various doors in life. Even when you are up for a job, you will earn more points than your competitors if you have excelled in multiple facets. For example, being street-smart and book-smart will increase your chances of being picked over someone with good marks but no experience.

Believe it or not, our world is run by people who are all-rounders. It is these all-rounders who reach the top of the world and apply their holistic strategies to make it better. Being multi-faceted makes you more equipped to deal with life and any challenges it might throw your way. But being an all-rounder, unlike being funny, is not a God-given gift. It is up to you to work on yourself and excel in multiple sectors. When it comes to personality-building and encompassing character-building, all of us need work. We can, fortunately, work hard to achieve this stature.

From my experience, here are a few methods you can try and things you can keep in mind to improve yourself.

1. Grab hold of that asset-liability list we have talked about so much. See your liabilities and work on turning them into your assets. The shift will also shift something in you.

2. Pick up hobbies; If you enjoy something and do it repeatedly, you will eventually improve yourself. You might start as a terrible singer, but with practice, you might turn decent or even good. And how cool would it be to tell people that you are a secret rockstar!

3. Notice the people around you and learn from them. Everyone you meet has something to teach you if you are willing to learn. If you think someone is kind, appreciate the quality and inculcate that in your character. A similar instance happened to me when I was at a DHL shipping office and wanted to ship a package overseas. The place was crowded, and everyone had a million queries, but the young gentleman (who reminded me of a college kid) behind the counter was ready to juggle them all. He was calm and collected, fielding the needs of everyone present. Even in such chaos, he managed to keep his professionalism intact. I ended up learning a lot from the situation.

4. And the last piece that has always helped me become a better person is trying my best to be "righteous" or "doing the next right thing." My mother was incredibly wise and caring and always led me down the correct path. This is why, before doing anything, I always think: "If my mother would approve, then it's God's Will".

CHAPTER 48

A SPLASH OF LEVITY

*"A splash might be a hint enough when being
soaked washes a good thing away."*

Whenever faced with any social situation, it is usually way too easy to turn serious and take everything at face value. Yet the true test of your maturity is when you know what needs to be dealt with solemnly and what should be taken with a splash of levity. In length, we have discussed the importance of humor in life and in enhancing your personality. However, is the same sense that tells you what should be taken lightly and how to do exactly that.

Not just so, but engaging your art of levity usually reflects well on your personality. It tells the world that you are mature enough not to take offense and throw tantrums in every serious situation. It also is a great indicator of your sense of humor and sportsperson spirit. Think of it as a recipe. When you love the art of cooking, you free-hand some of the measurements according to what you love. You might even want to experiment a little, permitting you to take things in a new direction. If not entirely new, then at least on a different tangent. Such an analogy can be applied to your charm of levity. Someone might expect you to jump on the chance, get angry, be serious, and many other things. But if you keep your cool and remember not to take yourself and the situation so seriously that it causes you anxiety, it will help you navigate life better.

Levity helps you enhance the situation you are already in, but know that it is not limited to the art of telling a joke either. Instead, it has everything to do with infusing humor in a situation and delivering it correctly. Do you remember the old-style lawn sprinklers with long, deliberate, high-swooping arcs whose pinhole streams of water lightly wetted the grass with each pass? The kind you put in the middle of the lawn and run back and forth under as a kid in the summertime. They would present enough water to the grass for it to be wet, but not enough that it would be drowning. Levity works in the same way. It might come as tasteless and crude if you try to be too funny.

Someone might assume you to be making light of the situation, not treating it with the respect it deserves. The failed attempt tends to leave an awkwardness in the air. Hence, the art of levity lies in its brevity.

Such subtle humor also has the power to be the binding agent that keeps the audience engaged in the conversation. Everyone likes to laugh; when done correctly, it can take away any boredom lingering in the atmosphere. Moreover, jokes and funny remarks have the power to wake a snoozing person's interest. It has a way of loosening people up, which will take a little pressure from the situation.

In Alcoholics Anonymous, one of the rules, Rule #63 taught stands to be—"Don't take yourself too damn seriously." Such a rule should be applied in all our lives. We love to think of ourselves as the center of attention. We have a shameless tendency to take ourselves way too seriously. We create our stress by wondering and worrying about every big or small situation. Yet, the minute we realize that we can't control everything on our own, we escape the need to be too serious. Every time you are faced with such a situation, ask yourself—"Is this worth getting upset about? Is it so important that I lose my peace over it?" When the roles are reversed, you know you do not wish to encounter someone so stiff and overly serious; such a person experiences trouble.

They are judgmental and unable to feel self-love, which is why we actively avoid being near such people. And when you know you don't even want to talk to someone like that, why would you want to be such a person? While it is not in our hands to control what happens in every single situation, you can still try to control how you react. Choosing not to take yourself way too seriously is a positive step toward dealing with negative situations that are out of your control. Limiting your need for reassurance can also be a great way to step back from every situation and realize how to behave. You do not need to be a people-pleaser and nor do you want to run after everyone for assurance. It is okay if someone dislikes you or is egging you on. Let it go!

CHAPTER 49

PATCHES OF LONELINESS

"Loneliness is not punishment, but an opportunity to climb from one place, into a new one."

In multiple cases, our desire to earn more and more stems from the world around us. "My neighbor's house is better than mine!" "My friend has a better job than I do!" "My brother earns more than me!"—jealousy is usually the biggest motivator that pushes us in the wrong direction. Yet, the only way this jealousy can ever be dealt with is not by gaining more than the other person but by filling the hole inside our hearts. We often disguise our true feelings with materialistic pleasures. We think a better job, more money, expensive jewelry, etc., will make us feel better enough to forget the pain we carry in our hearts. But obviously, it is not possible. When the serotonin of the short-lived material pleasure dies down, reality shows its face. Thus, the cycle goes on forever until we actively work on breaking it. This monumental issue, however, can easily be fixed if we turn to paying attention to ourselves rather than paying attention to others and our new possessions. If we face the loneliness inside, we can work on erasing it.

Loneliness is an inevitable part of the human journey. It is a feeling of emptiness that hardly anyone in the world has not experienced. Prolonged loneliness can manifest itself in mental and physical ailments, like depression, substance abuse, isolation etc. The only way out of any of these issues is by facing ourselves. The change we wish to see in the world starts with us. If we want the world to be nicer to us, we need to learn how to be nicer ourselves. "Knowing thyself", from the time of Socrates in ancient Greece, is the start that can take us to the ultimate destination of self-love and self-discovery,confidence, winning over our need for loneliness and depression. So, we can keep cursing loneliness, or start using it as a way of coming face to face with knowing our true selves.

"I'd love to change the world, but I don't know what to do". 10 Years After

After In one of the previous chapters, I asked you to make a list of two columns—one for your assets and one for your liabilities. When you are done making a list, you will have the things you wish to improve right in front of you. Dealing with issues when you know what they are is already half the job done. With such a list in front of you, you know the negative traits you want to diminish. Once you start doing that, you will realize that your love and respect for yourself are slowly but surely rising. Doing so is an excellent start to your self-love journey, which raises your confidence level. Saying so and achieving it are two different things, and I am aware of that. I would never preach something I didn't believe or wouldn't work. I, too, have struggled a lot with loneliness and running after useless goals to distract myself from the loneliness that resided inside me. I have never been married and have even been called commitment-phobic. All of us have the glaring liabilities that we wish wouldn't exist, yet the only way to make them disappear is by working on them. If you do not do so, you can keep collecting the seemingly-brilliant assets in life, but soon the shine will be gone, and the heart, again, will be empty. So, face the loneliness and slash it away to attain true happiness.

For some, success and personal victories sometimes bring unhappiness. When goals are met, then what? When I'm on a mission, it is inevitably about the challenge I seek that fuels me most. The chase is where the excitement is. You've heard "the thrill of the chase." So, the reward or the prize has little value when achieved.

CHAPTER 50

THE ULTIMATE GOAL

*"…what the behavior of men reveals as the purpose
and object of their lives, what they demand of life
and wish to attain in it. The answer to this can
hardly be in doubt: they seek happiness;
they want to become happy, and they remain so.
(Sigmund Freud, Civilization and Its Discontents)"*

Everything in life is done with one simple motive—happiness. No matter the action being carried out, whether it is getting a job that pays more, marrying someone, having kids, etc., everything is done to reach contentment. We work so that, we can relax and claim we are content. But life usually does not end up that way. With the challenges it throws our way, more often than not, we are struggling to deal with it and to find this 'happiness.' It eludes many people, and yet for some, it is easily available. Some can find this happiness in the simplicity of nature, and some cannot even find it in the heaviest bank accounts. Happiness is subjective that way, yet that does change its position in our hierarchical needs.

We often assume that unending happiness will fall in our lap after a life of struggle. If we suffer a lot, and pass through extreme challenges, then the end of the road must be hiding the key to happiness. We will arrive at our destination after maybe 10 or 20, or even 30 years of pain, and it will all have been worth it. Such a story looks great in movies and dramatic novels, but sadly, they are not always true to life. There is no eternal happiness nor a road that leads to it. This isn't Mario; you do not have to jump through hurdles to reach the castle holding your queen (happiness) hostage.

"Make today the best new day of your life."

Instead, the true happiness of life is present to you every day. You can be happy and content every day if you choose to be so. If you learn to accept things as they are and find happiness in the true essence of life, you will never be without a dose of happiness. Every day will be full of happiness, and you will string these days together to create a happy week, a happy month, and eventually, a happy life. Every 00:00 is an opportunity to start anew in every sector of your life. Even when you are worried about something, tell yourself that the new day will bring a new perspective. Time heals everything, it is true, but time also has the power to give you unlimited opportunities. Use these opportunities to change your outlook and measures of happiness.

Why do I feel fabulous today, and other times not so much so? As individuals, it's down to the combination of our physical makeup, that, and the flow in all our chemistry, and, of course, every outside force that exists, including people, places, and things. So, perhaps there's an abundance of goodness in your world right now for you. And only for now, because that moment could change as quickly as a shift in the wind. So many things must come together for things to be so good or bad. But the key is to not allow yourself to get too high or too low. The Boy Scout motto says it all here. "Be Prepared." Set boundaries. We often hear the saying, "life on life's terms," repeated. To be prepared and ready ourselves for the ways of the world. These counters enable us to stay in the middle of the bed as not to fall off.

Balance is arguably the mainstay for our ongoing happiness. If your start every day by looking at Elon Musk and being jealous of his wealth, you will never find happiness. But if you start every day by being grateful for what you already have while working on the goals you aim to achieve, contentment will be a your constant companion. Happiness is always everyone's ultimate goal, but do not blind yourself to its light. If you do, one day, you will wake up and realize that it had been with you all along, yet you were too busy mistaking something else for contentment.

CHAPTER 51

JUST TO BE FAIR

*"Today is yours for the taking—
so come and get it while you still can."*

The phrase remains the lesson of life to be incorporated every single day. Every day, we encounter decisions and choices. At that particular moment, they may not seem too monumental or life-altering, but every step we take creates a new path to walk on. Life also works in funny ways, and change usually does not announce its arrival. You can take a photo, upload it on Instagram, and the next day;, it could go viral, earning you thousands of followers and big names asking for a collaboration. Such instances have happened numerous times; lives have changed in the blink of a second, for better or worse. You have to be ready to accept it and stir it for your benefit. Being prepared is an underrated skill, but it needs to be understood where it is needed and where you need to jump in the pool to practice swimming. This book aims to train you in your most relaxed state. The lessons presented in the book are not to be implemented by you when the perfect opportunity arises, but ongoing and ever-consciously daily, creating the perfect opportunity if you consciously choose to follow the teachings of this book, it will teach you how to live your life. It will prepare you to take on every situation life can throw at you, even when you are not prepared to catch it. Or rather, "especially" when you are not prepared to catch it.

What surrounds us all is a world we share. Human nature and survival instincts may have stood in the way of equality. But, our innate and learned knowledge allows us to take what is rightfully ours in this existence. A brotherly allowance to take our fair share; everyone is entitled to a cut. People come from all over to live in the United States to gain freedom and rights. It's our freedom to have and follow our dreams.

CHAPTER 52

WHAT DO YOU REALLY NEED?

It comes down to... what do I need just for today?

"What do I need today?"—Every day we wake up, we ask ourselves this question. And the answer to it will enlighten our minds for the day, week, and life. Know that the question is not what we 'want' or 'desire,' but rather what we need. The differentiation is simple yet monumental and must be understood to lead a happier life. This answer, however, cannot be found in just one morning. Various mornings leading to different days are what it takes to learn this answer. With time we realize the differentiation between the two and figure out that what we truly need is very simple.

Before this realization comes to us, our materialistic nature wills us to run after the riches in life. We set out to buy as many things as our bank account allows us to find serotonin in them. At some point, we assume that happiness will come with a bigger car house or gems, but we realize the truth when we run through such instances,. It is maturity and experience that tells us that there is only one kind of happiness in the world, which resides within us and around us. If we want to be happy, we need to look at what we already have and find happiness. "I am happy where I am today!"—is the ultimate goal to be reached.

Our surroundings and upbringing also play a big part in shaping our desires and goals. Our materialistic world makes us think of happiness in terms of money and possessions, which is why we can turn misguided in life. However, when we turn away from the blinding light of money, we find that the universe has given us exactly what we need to survive. I once had an aunt born mentally challenged, yet I only saw her as a happy and carefree person throughout her existence. Until she passed away, she had made peace with who she was and was content with what she had. I believe some live in the only world they will ever know. Seeing them is sad, not in pity, but in all my ignorance to not recognize another's true happiness. Through her, I learned the valuable lesson I am sharing today—what we need is what we already have.

God doesn't give anyone everything, nor does he give no one nothing.

I have lived a life where I have been fortunate enough to own nice cars, yet today, you will see me driving a reliable, worry-free, small 4-door sedan. This shift happened when I realized I didn't need a sports car or a luxury one to fulfill my actual and honest needs. Now, when I come out of the grocery store, and there's a shopping cart (a buggy to you southerners) resting up against my driver's side door, I simply walk it to the carriage coral and hop in my car. No inspection, no problem. No problem because today's car is fine for today and a small dent won't make a dent in my day. When I am ready to worry again about where I park, I will get something a little fancier. An average car took me where I wanted to go comfortably, and I had to worry less about someone harming it while it was parked. It is usually maturity, experience, and the guidance of others that teach you this valuable lesson, as my aunt had unknowingly taught me. I strongly believe that for most of us, having had and lost is way more painful than never having had at all. To be born blind, the world they see is, again, the only one they've ever known. But to have seen the world we live in and then losing their sight of it is sad.

It is out of our selfishness that we collect and hoard, forgetting that it intends to make our life easier, not be our entire life. What brings us happiness is ourselves and the ones living around us. When we realize the true value of joy, we also understand that it comes from aiding the beings and the world around us. We try to help others and improve our society so it is a better world for everyone. Even in AA, the concept of "service work" is highlighted for all to follow, advising them to become better by engaging with the world around them.

Happiness is a subjective concept. But there are sure things in life that are bound to bring you peace and contentment. Being grateful for what you have and helping out in the world around you are sure ways of doing that. Even small actions can help because your simple action can make someone else's day. So, open your eyes to the world around you. Work on being grateful for it, and aim to make it better. That is what true happiness is.

CHAPTER 53

REGIMEN OVER ROUTINE

"Car & truck tires get stuck in ruts; get out and push yourself. It might be time to take a different road."

It is in our nature to strive for a set routine. Or it has been taught to us from a very early stage. In either case, the point remains that we have been brainwashed into believing that a routine is needed in life. Wake up, go to the office, eat food, watch TV, do this, and go to sleep to do it all over again tomorrow. Going through the same exercise to the point of monotony eventually blocks the flow of our creative juices. Such a routine can end up taking a negative toll on our minds. Our brains go into autopilot mode, and stimulation begins to wane. We become robot-like. This continuous routine, repeating itself to no end, can burn us out. It does get old and boring, and we find ourselves shifting into a subconscious state without even realizing it. When our mind wakes up and realizes how deep we have fallen, we want to escape it.

In contrast to routine, the solution presented to us is rather a regimen. Regimen does not dictate our activity at every minute of the day, but instead gives us a set of rules which we are to follow to make our life better. This regimen, hence, provides us with the freedom to do the things we want as our heart wishes, but it also keeps us on track with our values and ideals. It allows us to be true to ourselves no matter how we change our routines and activities. It allows us to preserve our creativity compared to the monotonous routine devised to kill it.

"Break out of the confines of your everyday humdrum routines. Take a chance on a new way. A new approach may bring better results you never knew were possible.

Pick up an activity in your routine and add 'regimen' at the end of it. When you realize it changes its meaning, you realize its importance. For example, when you go to the gym as a part of your routine, it becomes a chore you must do. Sometimes you do not want to go to the gym at all, but your routine says you need to do so, so you must. Yet, changing the way of going to the gym into a regimen of wanting to be fitter changes your outlook. You want to be fitter because you want to be a better you. If going to the gym does not suit your mind and body, you will find another way to stay fit. But the idea of staying fit will remain unchanged. In such ways, routine and regimen differ and can add a holistic viewpoint to your life; something routine cannot muster up.

You can alter the routine you have forced yourself to stick to in multiple ways. Even little things can end up adding jolts of meaning in your life, so it does not feel un-bearing burdensome. If you don't know what exactly you are to do, start with these:

- Be friends with nature: As I have already recommended, nature has healing powers that can make us feel at peace. We have deluded ourselves into believing that we are concrete animals, but the truth is that we thrive in nature. Various psychological studies also back up this claim, saying that nature has the power to ignite a creative fire in us and improving our mood. When you feel fresh and light, it is bound to energize you to perform your tasks well.

- Talk to your friends: We have discussed in lengths human beings as social animals, and it is the same reason why getting out of your solitude will be a way to break the monotony. All of us tend to wallow in our sorrows and trouble, yet talking to a loved one or a friend can lighten our hearts and make us feel heard. It does not matter if our friend cannot provide us with a solution. Just knowing that someone understands and is listening is sometimes enough.

- Break the monotony: Routines will always come with their share of boredom, and if you are in a position where you cannot change them completely, try altering them. The goal is to remove the monotony, so try adding new elements to your daily lives. Maybe you can start off by trying out new recipes or exploring a new place. The idea is to do something new and engaging every once in a life so you do not end up feeling stagnant.

CHAPTER 54

TIME FOR A CHANGE

*The key to life is finding someone or something
you like and then making it last.*

How often have you been in a situation where you are to do something you do not wish to do? It could be a job you hate or friends constantly passing condescending remarks at your expense. I am sure personal cases are popping up in your mind, but it has yet to be rectified because we let fear guide our minds and hearts. We force ourselves to show up to a job we hate because it brings us money. We let ugly remarks run off our backs because they are our only friends. We refuse to change our routine because cannot change our lives because of fear. We fear the change and how it will push us out of our comfort zone. It will make us stand face-front with a challenge, which will be an entirely new experience. Such change exposes us to new sceneries and perspectives, which, to think of it, seems too much to deal with. Especially when you have made peace with the horror of your comfort zone.

This book has provided you with different inputs and advice, some of you might already know and some that are completely new to you. Yet my prescription of the same does not result in an automatic action on your end. I have made a genuine case for every one of them, but there will still be readers who don't have it in them to follow through. They know it will improve their quality of life and living, but they still cannot do it. Why? The clear answer is fear.

If you are one of those, allow me to congratulate you. But before I do that, let me ask you—What is fear earning you? Why are you so attached to it? Even if you stay at a job you hate, it brings you no joy. You can earn the same amount of money at a different company. You might earn more when you get out of such a toxic environment and allow your creative juices to flow. So, what if you only have one friend? The world is out there, and you surely can make more. You have potential, but it will never be unlocked due to your fears. In the end, know that these fears are still doing nothing for you, so you might as well set out to see what awaits you on the other side.

If not you, then who? If not now, then when? Nobody else has the power to change your life. That much authority will always reside in you, which is why only you can access it. Like they say, "shoot for the moon, and you will land up in the stars." If you aim to change your life, it will get you out of your comfort zone. You might not instantly land where you wanted to be, but know it is okay. In life, success is always a long road. Do not let this crunch you back to your fears. Once you put out, the wonders of life are bound to provide you with something. If you aim for the moon, you might not end up there in one go, but at least you'll get out of the earth. And who knows, soon you will find the moon and maybe mars!

If there is a situation you do not like, you need to make your way out of it so you do not "get stuck." Everything in life can change; long-term, short-term, part-full, or full-time, but nothing is forever. This is why the exact change that drills fear in all of us needs to be our acquaintance, not the enemy. We need to think of it as a solution, not a problem. If you do not like your job, change it. If you do not like your house, change it. If you do not like where you live, change it. If you do not like your look, change it. If you are not happy with your partner, change it. Change is the solution, not the problem. Change is your way to peace. We all have goals and aims we hope to reach, so know that wherever you see yourself, change is the only vehicle that can take you there.

Let me present a scenario: You order a salad at a restaurant but with no onions or tomatoes. They bring you a salad that has both onions and tomatoes throughout. It's not what you wanted, but you pick out the onions and tomatoes you don't like, and now you're left with a salad that's essentially acceptable. I am not everything to everyone I want to be either, "I Didn't Ask to be Me," so I pick out the parts I don't like about myself, where change will make me a better person. Change doesn't necessarily mean different. It can point at or to "another level."

Life works similarly. You are given what you are given, which might not be what you asked for. How do you change that? Do you cry and crib about it, doing nothing ultimately, or will you get up and change what you do not like? We are given what we are given, but what we do with it is what matters. If we let fear guide us, we will sit in our seats and stare at a salad with onions and tomatoes. But if we accept change as the solution, we can remove them from our salad. So, are you daring enough to throw both out of your life?

CHAPTER 55

TEMPUS FUGIT—(TIME FLIES)

*"When you're young, everyone's old until
you're wise enough to understand why."*

I would love to say that "I have no regrets," but the more I think about it, the less realistic the statement becomes. "I should have done this or should have been there when I wasn't."—Many such thoughts also haunt me. Regrets are our shortcomings. They tell us where exactly we fall short in achieving our goal. They showcase our failures, putting us in front of it every day. So much so that they even ends up leading our life soon enough. They fill our days with contemplative thoughts and what-ifs, and before we know it, our entire life becomes an abyss we cannot dare climb out of. This is why it is essential to stop this at its very initial stage. Time is of the essence, and when it comes to regret, time flies too fast.

Was I too afraid to realize something that I am fully capable of but didn't have the fortitude or enough faith in myself at the time? We can alleviate entertaining this dilemma from happening if we take a leap of faith once in a while. Nike's most famous saying: "Just Do It," is forever lasting and words we can all easily remember. Another famous quote…

> "Don't put off until tomorrow what you can do today"
> —Ben Franklin

Time has the power to fly past us too quickly. One minute we are a kid playing in a park, and the next, we pass one on our way to work. When we are kids, we have no worries; nothing in the world matters to us. When we enter our teens and 20s, our focus turns to enjoying our moment; we are young and carefree, so we must live life to the fullest. Finally, in our 30s, we are beginning to get hold of a serious life where new challenges are ready to face us. No matter what age, we constantly push ourselves thinking, "That's nothing! I have plenty of life left to live!" But before you know it, you are 40 or 50, and soon more than half of your life is over.

Today, I am 61, and the younger ones view me as someone really old. Some might even be right in thinking so, because I have lived almost 70-80% of my life. All of us have our timelines given by God and have a set time limit on us. This time limit can either make us work harder to enjoy the limited time we have, or it can push us into a dread of dying. As I have mentioned multiple times in this book, life is what you make of it. Everything you need to live a brilliant life and market yourself as an excellent individual is right in your hands. You are your brand, and the world awaits to witness your glory. Will you put on a show for them, leaving them in admiration, or will you fizzle out when nobody looks? The choice, as the book has taught you, is yours.

I present aging in a very honest and pleasant way. By God's design (or my creator in my case), I believe he eases us out of this world gently and gradually in most cases so that we don't freak out about never being around again, to do more things. Can you imagine the anxiety and worrying some people might experience if they knew that exact day?

Eventually, we all come back down to earth and a life of simplicity. I still like rock and roll, but I also listen to the music my dad did. It not only brings back memories of my youth, but admittedly can be soothing when I need to be peaceful. We grow old until we stop growing and are moved out. We don't freak out, yet finally, it is our time.

END STATEMENT

It's okay to laugh out loud (LOL) when you're all
alone, but the cause for it must be real.

Laugh—live longer.